Stories From
Sharon
and Her
Service Dog
Charley

SHARON WINTERS

For information about this title or to order other books
and/or electronic media, contact the publisher:
Sharon Winters
Chandler, Arizona
www.SharonWinters.com

Printed in the United States of America

ISBN: 979-8-9895372-2-8 (hardcover)
ISBN: 979-8-9895372-3-5 (softcover)
ISBN: 979-8-9895372-4-2 (eBook)

Library of Congress Control Number: 2025921833

Cover photos by Hatton Pet Portrait Studio

Editor: Colleen C. Eagle
Cover and Interior Design: Sandra Jones,
EagleLadyDesignStudio.com

Dedicated to

Brittie and Jesse Lyon
Thank you for saving Charley so he could live his best life.

Maricopa County Animal Care and Control
Mesa, Arizona

Phoenix Dog Training: Will Bangura
Phoenix, Arizona
Thank you, Will, for training Charley to be the perfect service dog he is today. Were you really raised by wolves?

Thank you also to Jordan Marsteller at Phoenix Dog Training for helping to train Charley and introducing him to whipped cream.

Other Books Written by Sharon Winters

Cutted Chicken in Shanghai
Karl's Diary: It's a Dog's Life

Children's Picture Books
Runtie the Desert Rat
A Quilt for Charley: Based on a True Story

Contents

Sharon's Stories page 1

This collection of vignettes begins with Sharon's childhood exposure to new languages and fascinating people. Her memorable encounters feature strange foods, travel adventures, errant children, funny pets, and a beloved granddaughter.

Charley's Stories page 31

Charley's doggy journal captures his experiences (and opinions) as a shelter dog adopted into a life of service, all told from his point of view, and enhanced through colorful photos and illustrations.

Bonus Stories and Interviews page 89

"About Sharon Winters' Books" introduces Sharon's previous four books, along with an unpublished story featuring the golden-eyed Boykin Spaniel, Karl. The deeper story behind Sharon's motivation to write her Chinese cultural memoir is also revealed.

"About Sharon Winters' Writing: *Authority Magazine* Interview" gives readers an insightful look into the craft of writing from Sharon's unique position as an award-winning author and humorist.

I am thankful for laughter, except when milk
comes out of my nose.
— Woody Allen, American actor, comedian, and filmmaker

A dog is the only thing on earth that loves you
more than you love yourself.
— Josh Billings, 19th century American humorist

FOREWORD

"When I look into the eyes of an animal, I do not see an animal, I see a living being, I see a friend, I feel a soul." I once quoted these words (by A.D. Williams) when writing about the friend whose story brought Sharon and I together. That story, penned back in 2008 for the *MENSA Bulletin*, recounted a meeting with a petite lady who found herself stranded, alone and pregnant, in a post office parking lot on a brisk and snowy afternoon. Clearly, her day had not gone as she'd planned—or hoped. And, thanks to her, neither did ours. Well, ours didn't go as planned, I mean. For, had we known what love and wonder were about to be revealed, and the other very special meetings this one would inspire, surely both my husband and I would have been hoping, our whole lives, this day might come.

As it happened, this fascinating lady was a pet rat—a form that could have stopped us from opening our home—and hearts—to her, and one which quite possibly stopped at least a few readers from fully appreciating the value of her friendship. But, hours after the magazine hit mailboxes, I received an email response to my article—from Sharon. Though fellow Mensans, we were, at the time, total strangers . . . and yet not. Before I'd even finished reading the full message, along with the attachments she'd included (stories written from the perspective of two guinea pigs), it was clear we were kindred spirits. "You, too," she later said, "know what animals think."

Knowing what animals think—much like knowing what other humans think—is largely a matter of listening. It's also being open to possibility, and seeing beyond what appears, into what truly is. It's hearing a creature without speech speak, on a level in which words are useless, anyway. In short, it's about love.

So, too, are the stories that comprise this book. Through brief glimpses into the moments, big and small, that fill a life, we're shown what it means to make a life full—regardless if that life belongs to a human, a guinea pig, a chicken, a pet rat . . . or a dog—one whose best years, some might think, were already behind him, when he learned the life of his dreams was really about to begin.

While the book is divided into two sections, and shares two individual perspectives, both underscore the fullness of a love-filled life—and the unexpected surprises that can pepper the journey—from how "pain" can lead to the gift of a painting by a famous artist to the simple pleasures of a quilt and a warm washcloth.

Both sections, of course, feature the same family members, and detail the ways in which their separate and common encounters bring both Sharon and Charley joy. Weaved throughout, we see the joy Sharon and Charley bring each other. As one of Charley's trainers said, "In all my time of training dogs, I've never seen a dog who loved someone as much as Charley loves Sharon."

This love he clearly feels in return—and it constantly assures him, "All is right with the world."

—Mil Scott, editor and publisher of *The Rodent Reader Quarterly*

PREFACE

Home is the place where love is found—that feeling of wholeness, belonging, and comfort. I am fortunate that l find love wherever I am. It follows me and finds me. I am never alone.

When I lived in Shanghai, China, my Chinese friends were always there for me. Sometimes I didn't even know their names, and they entered my life for only minutes. Others have become lifelong friends like Stella, Gao, and Jin.

In Berlin, there was a honey bee that befriended me, and a doctor who treated me for pneumonia.

In my life I have lived in many U.S. states and called them home. I live with a loving and wonderful husband, and my children are living their own lives.

But the greatest constant in my life has been the many pets I have had. They are sentient beings who are always here for me. Even those that have passed on are still held in my heart. Not a day goes by when I don't think of Wolfgang, Jake, Karl, Bacon, and so many others that have passed on.

As I sit here in my living room, my husband is reading the newspaper, and Charley, our latest rescue from Maricopa County Animal Care and Control in Arizona, is lying beside me watching my every move. When I get up to make lunch, he will sit just outside the kitchen and stay out of my way as I move from the sink, stove, counter, and refrigerator. He knows he will get pieces of London broil as a reward for staying out of my way.

For my husband—and for me—Charley now completes our family. The air we breathe is filled with his love and loyalty.

This book talks about Charley and the other people who have completed my life with love and laughter and those times in my life that have made my life worth living.

Much thanks goes to my editor and friend, Colleen Eagle. What a pleasure it is to work with you. It was a happy day when I met you at a Mensa convention.

Much thanks also goes to Sandy Jones, a wonderful designer who understands those technological things I hope to never have to learn.

And to Colleen and Sandy, thank you both for putting my book out there for readers who want to step into my world for a moment and to hear the voice of a dog.

In the Beginning . . .

My parents and I lived in a one bedroom basement apartment in Chicago. The "Chicago L," the elevated transit system, was behind our building, and I loved the sound of its rumbling as it whooshed by our apartment.

When I was three years old, my mother went back to work, and I stayed at the Kaminsky's apartment during the day. They lived in a nearby walk-up fourth floor apartment. My parents knew the Kaminsky family because they owned our apartment building.

The Kaminsky family escaped Poland after Hitler invaded in 1939. A large picture of their family hung on

Four years old in Chicago.

the wall of their apartment. They had ten children, but I only ever saw three of them. I don't know what happened to the other seven. Margaret, their youngest child, was fourteen. She lived with her parents along with an older sister who worked in Chicago during the day.

Everyone in the family was kind to me. Margaret often took me to Lake Michigan where I learned to swim. At the Lake there were steps going into the Lake. The water was green, and Margaret told me not to drink it. No problem there!

Mrs. Kaminsky was a great cook and meticulous housekeeper. When she made bread a few times a week, she would open a window, which had no screen, and put the bread on

Run Margaret, Run!

the window sill to cool. And to clean her windows, her one remaining son would come over and lean out the window. Mrs. Kaminsky would shut the window on his legs while he washed the outside of the windows. I was terrified!

At lunchtime Mr. Kaminsky would come home. Margaret and Mrs.

Kaminsky spoke to me in English, but during lunchtime, Polish, Yiddish, and Russian were spoken. Somehow, as the months went by, I began to understand these other languages. One day during lunch, Mrs. Kaminsky commented to Mr. Kaminsky that I was a chatterbox! I was surprised to hear that, and I said, in Polish, "*Nie jestem gadula!*" "I am not a chatterbox!" There were raised eyebrows and silence at the table.

The Chatterbox.

When I was almost five years old, we moved to a German-Italian neighborhood in a Chicago suburb. What I found most interesting about the Italian language were the hand gestures that went along with the words, and I still remember them. But I soon

learned to never use any of those gestures at school, or my parents would be called by the principal. I'm not even going to say in English what some of those gestures meant.

I will still occasionally slip in an Italian, Yiddish, or other foreign word when speaking to my friends or my husband. They can always figure out what I mean. For example, when I want to remind my husband to feed our dog Charley, I know if I say "Charley" or "dog" or "dinner" or several other words, Charley knows what I'm saying and will start drooling on the floor, or come over to me, give me the "look," and drool on my leg. So I might say, "Honey, it's time for *pasquale* to eat."

Sometimes it's good to know words in foreign languages. I was working at a law firm and the printer stopped printing. When I opened a door to the inside of the printer, I saw a word etched onto a metal bar. The word was "*Achtung*" (watch out)! Hmmm . . . I closed the door of the printer and looked for someone else to fix it. I wasn't going to touch the inside of that printer.

For me, it was a remarkable childhood. Too bad my parents only spoke English.

Charley

Berlin Pizza

Before I say anything else about my vacation to Berlin in 2014, I should tell you that (1) I don't like German food, and I knew that before I agreed to go to Berlin with my husband, and (2) Ten days before this trip, I decided I should brush up on my German since I only remembered a few sentences and how to call someone a "dumbbell." I got a cheat sheet for German grammar and learned three hundred German words using an app on my phone.

On our first full day in East Berlin, we bought pizza from a street kiosk. My thought was, how can anyone ruin pizza? This isn't even a traditional German food. I took one bite of this flaccid slice of pizza and almost threw up. It was covered with jalapeño seeds. Really?! This was their idea of pizza? The word *idioso* came to mind as well as a certain Italian gesture. I guzzled some water and hoped to put out this fire. I couldn't even feel the water going over my tongue. And then I thought, aha! The perfect fix for this fire on my tongue would be ice cream.

Armed with my cheat sheet and three hundred German words, I sniffed around a couple of streets until I found an ice cream parlor where I ordered *"Kakoa Eis Creme."* My favorite. The server behind the bar took a teaspoon and put a dollop of chocolate ice cream in a paper cup. He handed me a tiny flat wooden spoon. I hadn't seen a spoon like this since the days of the Good Humor Man. When he tried to hand me my ice cream, I put my hand up and said, *"Mehr, bitte."* "More, please."

He added one more tiny scoop of ice cream. These two scoops of ice cream were so small that I could put one scoop of ice cream in each eye, and it wouldn't even hurt. When he tried to hand me this cup of ice cream, I said, *"Mehr, bitte."*

He added one more scoop of ice cream into the cup and handed it to me as he said, *"Das ist alles, die was in diesem becher passt."* "This is all I can fit into this cup."

Think quick! How do I say, "Then get a bigger cup!"

The cost was €6. That's $7.98 to us Yankees.

Berlin Doors

I find doors fascinating. The most interesting door I saw had a boulder blocking its entrance. The boulder is in front of the door to a five-story bunker used during World War II. It is located in Berlin in the Reinhardtstrasse area. It is now an art gallery.

Visitors to this art gallery aren't challenged to try rock climbing. Other doors to the building provide an unobstructed entrance.

Berlin Bees

While still in Berlin, I learned that this city has a honey bee propagation and protection program. There were bazillions of bees everywhere. I saw a lot of them crawling all over bakery goods and anything else they sensed might be sweet. I must say that they never bothered me and were well mannered. They buzzed around in a purposeful and Zen-like way as they chanted to themselves.

Yesterday, however, one bee gently landed on my shoulder and said, "Do you mind if I rest here? I am not feeling well."

"I am sorry to hear that," I said. "What happened?" And the bee said, "I ate some bad pizza."

A Dog Story

While walking from my car to work, I saw a cute dog with its owner. I said, "Oh! Is that a Jack Daniel?" The owner responded, "Do you need a drink? This is a Jack Russell!"

Three Southern Belles

Here's one of my favorite jokes.

Three Southern Belles were talking about what they received for their anniversaries. The first Belle said, "My husband gave me his credit card and said to buy whatever I wanted!" The two other Belles said, "Isn't that nice!"

The second Southern Belle said, "My husband gave me a brand-new Cadillac!" The two other Belles said, "Isn't that nice!" And they each turned to the last Southern Belle who said, "My husband bought etiquette lessons for me!"

The two Southern Belles were puzzled as one asked, "Well . . . What did you learn?" And she said, "I learned to say, 'Isn't that nice!' instead of 'I really don't give a damn.'"

My husband knows this joke, so when I tell him, "Isn't that nice," he knows exactly what I mean.

Classroom Skeleton

We were sitting in a classroom that had a skeleton in a case with a glass front. About a hundred of us were waiting for our Constitutional law professor to start our class. The professor was a serious man, void of a sense of humor. We were all bored out of our minds with nothing to do while time ticked by, and we knew we were in for another long lecture that we would be tested on for the bar exam.

Two young men—brilliant future attorneys—took the skeleton out of his resting place, rolled him to the podium, and placed his bony hands on the law professor's podium. His skull leaned toward the microphone. Jaws that were slightly open showed perfect teeth.

I said, "Let's tape a sign on the podium that says, '1946 Hide-and-Go-Seek Champion!'"

Too late. In walked the professor. "Somebody put this skeleton back!" he roared.

Sigh . . . Some people are no fun.

Never Say "No" in China

My husband and I lived in Shanghai, China, for two years, and I attended Fudan University where I intensively studied the Chinese language and culture. I learned that it's okay to say, "I'm sorry," but it is never okay to say, "No." If you say "No," either in English or a Chinese dialect, you will be perceived as a brute.

The Chinese say "No" in many other ways. This is a culture that does not want to embarrass someone or cause someone to lose face, and it is a culture in which people aim for cooperation.

One way to say "No" is to say: "不方便的, *Bù fāngbiàn de*" [Boo-fahng-be-enn-duh]. This literally means "(This is) not convenient." Another way to say "No" is by saying you will study the matter: "研究研究, *Yánjiū yánjiū*" [YAN-ge-Oo]. This literally means, "(I will) study, study." Another way to say "No" is to say, "(I) will do my best" by saying: "(我)会尽我所能, *(Wǒ) huì jîn wǒ suônéngz*" [who-AY-jin wa-SUE-OH NUNG].

Those phrases were useful to me, especially on one occasion with a Chinese friend. She came to visit me in Shanghai, and because I was a jeweler, I had catalogs of jewelry from U.S. businesses at my apartment. While we were sitting at my dining room table, she began looking through one of the catalogs.

As she browsed through the catalog, she wrote down a list of ten pieces of jewelry that she wanted. She passed the list to me and said in Mandarin, "I would like for you to bring these items back for me the next time you go to the States."

I took her list in my hand and quickly figured out that these ten pieces would cost me over five thousand dollars. I said, "会尽我所能." "I will do my best." She smiled and accepted my gentle "No." And the subject was never brought up again.

From Beijing With Love

Because I lived in Shanghai for two years and studied Chinese at Fudan University, I speak Mandarin, and for many years after I returned to the United States, I would go back to China to buy pearls from pearl farmers I knew. I was getting ready to sell pearls from my shop in High Point, North Carolina, and didn't have time to make about fifty pounds of pearls into jewelry before the next Furniture Trade Show in North Carolina. And so I thought, I'll just take these pearls to Ling Ling's shop in Beijing, and her stringers will get it done in about five days. I had ten thousand dollars in cash in my purse—mostly singles—which at the time was the legal limit to take out of the U.S. Oops—the legal limit to bring cash *into* China was six thousand dollars.

I had no problem leaving the U.S. with my pearls in one bag and my clothes in another bag. Over twenty hours later I landed in Beijing. I knew my friend, Mr. Gao, would be waiting for me at the airport.

I arrived in customs, and a Chinese agent lifted my bag with the pearls and gave me "the look." Talking to himself in Mandarin, he said, "What the hell

is in here?!" He threw my bag onto an x-ray machine, and the pearls lit up like a bomb of a million M&M's® chocolate candies exploding. And I thought, "Oh, that's so pretty."

He called me over to an area where luggage is inspected. Four customs agents descended upon me and my two bags. There was a large glass window in front of me. I could see Mr. Gao's head popping up and down. I knew he was worried. He was trying to see what was going on. I began to chant in my head: The world is a friendly place.

Opera length pearls adorn my dress, a Chinese quipao.

After searching my two pieces of luggage, an agent said in English, "How much you pay?!"

I knew he was asking me the cost of the pearls, so I quoted him the price I'd paid to purchase them from Ling Ling Jewelry. They asked me this same question many times, and I repeated the same answer. (I went to law school and worked in a law firm. I know how the game is played. Never change your answer.) One customs agent found a plastic bag full of necklace clasps with a sticker on the bag that said "Korea." They asked me if I had been to Korea. They were trying to catch me in a lie. They searched my passport for a visa from Korea. I didn't have one.

A young guy said in English, "You have import license?" I said no. They began to discuss what to do with me. They didn't know I knew what they were saying. Gao's head continued to bob up and down. I waved to him. I turned to an agent and asked, "Can my friend come in here?"

Bins of unstrung pearls at Ling Ling's jewelry store.

He said, "No! No friend! We check purse now." He pulled out the thick envelopes of money from my bank and looked in one and said, "Whaaaaaa!" He quickly put all the envelopes back and said, "You take!" as he gave my purse back to me without counting the money.

The four agents sounded like bees as they kept repeating, "太多了。 *Tai dou le!*" "Too many!"

The youngest guy of the four agents finally said in English, "Okay. We put in storage. You leave China. You pick up." He motioned for me to leave with one suitcase and my purse. This meant that I would have to buy more jewelry from Ling Ling with a credit card tomorrow for the upcoming trade show and string my fifty pounds of pearls myself into jewelry. I would have to sell those pearls at some future trade show.

Gao was relieved to see me walk out of customs. I greeted him in a traditional Chinese manner, with my hands pressed together, and he then slapped his wrists together as he said in Mandarin, "I thought they were going to handcuff you and throw you in prison!"

My friend, Mr. Gao.

I smiled as I spoke to my dear friend in Mandarin, "Gao, the world is a friendly place."

Gao looked at me with a puzzled expression as he shrugged his shoulders. He took my luggage and said, "好。我们吃吧" "Okay. Let's eat."

I told him how happy I was to see him, and he said in Mandarin, "I'm so glad to not have to visit you in prison." We both laughed, and he again spoke to me in Mandarin, "I know. The world is a friendly place."

Miguel Zapata (1940–2014)

On a flight in 1986 from Dallas, Texas, where I lived at the time, I heard the man sitting behind me order a beer in Spanish. While my Spanish is passable, I often get words mixed up in the languages that I know, including my native tongue, English. For example, I get *Janice* and *Janet* mixed up, *Rich* and *Rick*, and *subscription* and *prescription.* Sometimes I'll mix in Spanish words with French words and Mandarin words. It's embarrassing.

When the flight attendant asked the man to give her four dollars for the beer he ordered, he just shrugged his shoulders, and I heard him say in Spanish that he didn't speak English.

The flight attendant called out, "Does anyone speak Spanish?"

I raised my hand, and she asked me to ask him to give her four dollars.

I unfastened my seat belt and turned around. As I leaned over the seat, I suddenly remembered that I often mix up the Spanish words for *dollar* and *pain*, which are *dolar* and *dolor*. Not wanting to embarrass myself, I said, "*Señor*, give her four bucks . . . *por favor.*"

Everyone in my section burst out laughing, and he gave the flight attendant four dollars.

You would think that after this I would study those words again so I could remember them for the next time I needed them. But no.

Back in Dallas, I went to an art supply store to buy some frames. I waited my turn behind an unfamiliar man standing at the counter speaking to the cashier in Spanish. She kept telling him that she couldn't understand what he was saying, and he kept repeating what he was trying to tell her. Finally, I spoke up and said to her, "I can help him. He wants mat board."

The clerk called her manager and told him that this man wanted mat board and that he didn't speak English. She looked toward me as she told the manager that I would help him. The manager opened a door on the side of the shop and the three of us entered a narrow room with top-to-bottom shelves of mat board.

I held out my hand to the wall with mat board and told him in Spanish to choose whatever he wanted.

After he looked at several shelves, he pulled out some gray mat board and asked me in Spanish for the price.

I looked at the manager as I said, "He wants to know how much this mat board costs." The manager said it was $1.30. I looked at the Spanish-speaking artist and told him the price in Spanish; at least, I thought I told him the price.

The artist smiled as he said for me to hold out my hand. He put thirty cents in my hand and then pinched my butt. Oh, no! In a flash I realized I had mixed up my Spanish word for *dollar* with the word for *pain*! We both laughed when I realized I had told him the mat board was "one *pain* and thirty cents."

The following week I returned to the art store, and when I saw the cashier, she said, "Hi, Sharon! Miguel Zapata left something for you."

I was puzzled. "Who is Miguel Zapata?"

She said, "He is a famous Spanish artist, and he's in Dallas for an art show at Southern Methodist University. He left some artwork for you and wrote a message to you in Spanish." She reached under the counter and pulled out his artwork and handed it to me. "Sharon, what did he say?"

As I held the artwork in my hand, I read the message: "For Sharon with all my gratitude and kindness."

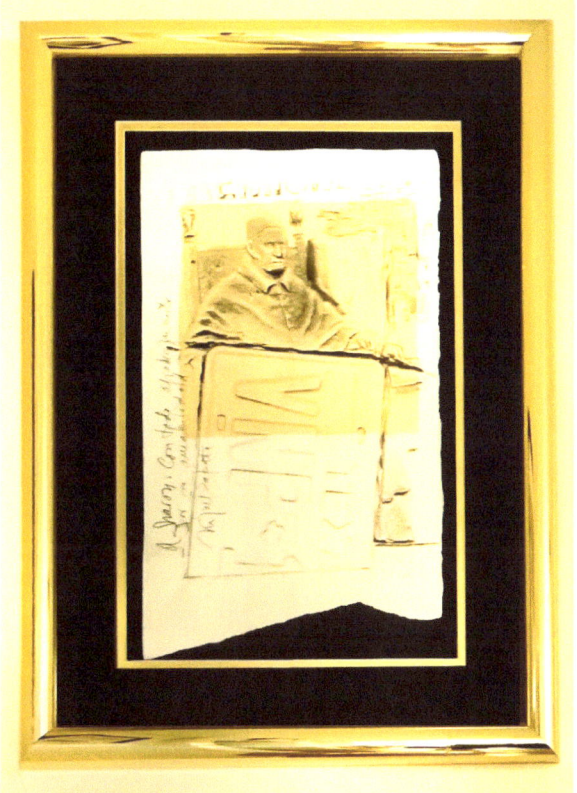

Artist Miguel Zapata pressed wet watercolor paper over a Texas license plate, then painted the subject with watercolors after the paper was dry.

Wow! I never know whom I will meet. His artwork can sell for thousands of dollars—or is it pains?!

Guinea Pig Kisses

What is better than rubbing noses with a Guinea Pig? When I was in college, living in my own apartment, I had to have a fur-child. I went to a pet shop and found a cute Guinea Pig. I called her Bacon because she reminded me of a Hampshire pig with a white band around her tummy. She was smart and learned several tricks for which she was rewarded with treats of fruit. She loved blueberries, bananas, and strawberries.

I taught her to count to three. I would hold up one, two, or three fingers, and that's how many times she would touch my nose. I called those nose touches "Guinea Pig kisses." I also taught her to turn in a circle. She was treat motivated. And when she was especially happy, she would popcorn: she would jump up and turn around. She also loved Latin music. When she heard this music, she would chutter, back up, and wiggle her butt.

Later, when I was married and living in a house, I added a dog to our family. He was a Flat Coated Retriever, and his name was Jubel. I kept Bacon in a kitty litter pan, which I placed on a raised TV tray at the end of the couch. Jubel and Bacon got along and would often touch noses.

Bacon and Sharon.

Whenever I would open the refrigerator door, Bacon would wheek and wheek until I gave her some lettuce. She lived for nine years and now lives in my heart.

Big Red

Big Red and Sharon.

We lived on a ranch, and I added more animals. I had a horse, a rabbit, and two dogs, so why not add chickens? I had a chicken coop built and ordered a dozen chicks from the feed store. As they grew, I noticed there was one rooster. I heard that roosters could be mean, so I was determined that we would be friends. Every day I would pick him up and have a talk with him. Soon, when he would see me, he would come up to me and expect to be picked up and hear sweet words. He was a yard boss but a sweetheart when he was in my arms.

Lucky Duck

While living in Texas, I took a job as a teacher in a middle school in a San Antonio barrio. I was dubbed "Resource Teacher." That meant special education. Students were sent to my class for one or two hours a day for help with their studies. In this school, all of the students spoke Spanish and English. I was probably hired because I had a teacher's license in learning disabilities and could speak Spanish.

One of my students, Carlos, thought I was the luckiest person he had ever known. No matter what I said was going on in my life, Carlos would say, "You are a lucky duck."

When I said I was late to work because the battery to my car died, he said, "You have a car?! You are a lucky duck." When I said I hadn't had time to vacuum my apartment all week, he said, "You have an apartment?! You are a lucky duck!" Was there anything I could say that would get me any sympathy from him?

After work one day, I was riding my bike when the front wheel slid onto some gravel. There was a blue truck parked on the side of the road. I fell sideways into this truck. First I hit my head on the truck door, and then my bike and I continued our slide onto the pavement. My forehead, hand, and knee were bleeding.

The next day I limped into work. Carlos would be coming into my classroom in the afternoon. After lunch, I sat at my desk with secret and internalized glee. I looked forward to Carlo's shock and sympathy as he walked in the door to my room and up to my desk to hand in his homework. I had practiced a sad and painful face before coming to work. I had also left my wounds clean but unbandaged for the best effect. They looked awful.

Carlos appeared at the right side of my desk as the school bell rang for classes to start. As he set down his worksheet, he looked at my pathetic face. "Ms. Winters, what happened?!"

"Oh, Carlos," I said, with a tremor in my voice, "I fell into a truck!" I moved my hair away from my eye. Carlos stared at the goose egg on my forehead. He raised his eyebrows in surprise.

"And then Carlos, I slid down the street. I hurt my hand stopping my fall, and I scraped my knee. There was blood all over the street!"

Carlos looked at my scraped hand. I was wearing a dress, and I stretched out my leg with great pain and said, "My leg was all bloody, too."

Carlos looked at my knee and said, "*Hijole!* How did you fall?"

"Carlos, I was riding my bike after work."

Carlos smiled as he said, "You have a bike?! You are a lucky duck!"

I wonder what Carlos is doing with his life. Since Carlos, I have never met another person with such a positive attitude. Some students, like Carlos, changed my life.

I hope you are well and happy, Carlos. I'm a lucky duck to have met you.

Your Life Will Be Good

As an ESL (English as a second language) teacher for the Dallas Independent School District, I worked with Spanish-speaking students. Most of the parents of my students didn't speak English, and I often visited my students' homes to talk with their parents. My students all knew that if anyone ever gave me a problem, I could drive to their home and talk to their mother or father. My students were angels.

I had office hours when students could get extra help or just talk about what might be bothering them. My "office" was in the teacher's lounge, which was a large room.

One day there was a knock on the door. A teacher in the lounge opened the door, and I heard Juan say, "I need to speak with Ms. Winters."

I invited Juan to sit next to me at a table. Juan was sixteen years old, and he had some papers in his hand. As he sat next to me, he said, "The principal said I can drop out of school, and you need to sign these papers." He placed the papers on the table for me to sign. I knew his mother, and I thought to myself: If you don't at least graduate, the world will eat you alive, not to mention what your mother will do to you.

I said, "Okay. First let's see what jobs you can get." There was a *Dallas Morning News* on the table, and I turned to the section that listed job openings. As we looked at the postings, the other teacher in the room was smiling and listening intently to us while she pretended to read a newspaper.

After looking for jobs, Juan thought he could work at a restaurant cooking burgers. I said, "When you work for an hourly wage, then you have to pay taxes, social security, and get medical insurance because this job doesn't have any benefits. And since your mom and dad are paying for your meals and for a place for you to stay, you should pay your mom at least fifty dollars a week. Your medical insurance could be two hundred dollars or more a month. So, you'll get maybe forty dollars a day after you pay taxes and social security alone." As I did the math on a piece of paper, Juan looked concerned.

"Juan, do you have a car to get to work?" I knew he didn't. When he shook his head no, I said, "You can take the bus to work. That's not expensive. But let's look and see how much cars cost."

I opened the classified ads. "Oh, Juan! This car is only five thousand dollars. It probably won't need a lot of repairs for a year or so. Gas isn't real expensive right now. And remember to get car insurance and pay your license fee every year. Do you want to see how much apartments are?"

Juan shook his head no. My fellow teacher now hid her face behind her newspaper. I'm sure she was feeling entertained.

By the time I finished with the newspaper, I had Juan living with his parents until he was forty, taking his girlfriend on a bus ride to a cheap restaurant for a date, and not being able to afford either medical or car insurance.

"Juan, I just had my car fixed, and the mechanic who fixed my car started his job at fifty thousand dollars a year."

Juan said, "*Vaja?*" "Really?"

I reached for the papers he wanted me to sign. Juan said yes when I asked him if he liked cars. "How about if you take automotive repair classes?"

Juan smiled for the first time since coming in to talk with me. I wrote on the top of Juan's dropout papers: Please sign Juan up for automotive classes today.

Juan stood up, and I handed him the papers that would change his life for the better. When I speak to students in their first language, those words go to their heart. I said, "*Tu vida será buena.*"

Juan told me thank you and gently closed the door behind him.

The other teacher in the room put the newspaper down on her lap and was almost laughing as she said, "Oh! That was rich! What did you say to him in Spanish?"

"I said, 'Your life will be good.'"

Pregnancy Vocabulary

I was pregnant, and I felt horrible! AND I was hungry. What made me feel worse was riding in a car. One morning while riding with my husband, our route took us through restaurant row. I yelled to him, "Stop the car!" Of course, he asked why. That was not a good thing to say.

It's unfortunate that it took him months to learn the pregnancy vocabulary, which offers three suitable responses for most situations: "Okay," "Yes dear," and "I'm sorry." The correct response that day was "Okay."

I told my husband again, "Pull over. I have to eat something NOW!" He pulled over in front of a French restaurant. I snapped my seat belt off, and my quiet husband helped me out of the car.

Inside the restaurant we were seated at a two-top with a white tablecloth that I considered taking a bite out of. Because this was a French restaurant, the menu listed a variety of quiches. I actually spoke French, so I understood the words on the menu.

I felt so miserable and hungry I was ready to lie on the floor, have my husband feed me, and stay there until I delivered my baby. We were given ice water, which I drank without taking a breath. I clunked the empty glass down on the table like I was in a bar on a Western movie set.

A waitress appeared with her pen poised over a pad of paper. Being a gentleman, my husband motioned to me to be first to give her my order. As he was taking a drink of water, I pointed to what

His first word was "Mommy."

I wanted on the menu and said, "I want a French Quickie."

My husband spat water all over the white tablecloth. How did that waitress keep a straight face?

Parenting Tip

When I was a new mother, I read many books about raising children, and they were frequently of no help with my oldest son. When Mikie wanted something, and I wasn't going to let him have it, I would reason with him. That never worked. He wanted what he wanted, and that's that. But one day when Mikie was about four years old, I finally found something that worked. We were shopping in a mall, and he saw a toy blue truck he wanted.

"Mom, would you buy me that blue truck?"

"No, Mikie, we aren't buying any toys today."

"Why, Mom?! Why can't you buy me that truck? I really want that truck!"

Mikie was getting close to a blowout. I knew the signs. Just then something popped into my weary mother's mind, and I knew exactly how to stop him from continuing with his temper tantrum. I put my hand on my hip to help me feel powerful and said, "Mikie, you can't have that truck or any other toy today because I'm a mean mother, and I don't want you to be happy."

Mikie looked at me with great surprise and was well behaved for the rest of the day.

Another Parenting Tip

There are books that only require the reading of the title to know the entire message of the book. One such example is: *Do What You Love and the Money Will Follow*. There's no need to read that book! My youngest son, T-Bone, will tell you that while good parents raised him, his mother—that would be me—had a shortcoming, which was that I was a lousy disciplinarian.

T-Bone's dad, however, could get T-Bone to do whatever T-Bone was supposed to be doing, and he did this without ever raising his voice or even threatening to hit T-Bone. (I never saw my husband get angry or even heard him let out a "bad" word.) He would tell T-Bone what he was supposed to be doing, and there would quickly be dust behind T-Bone's heels. To me, this was magical. How did he do that?! I set off in search of a book that would tell me the magical secret of disciplining children. There was no such book. But if there was such a book, it would be called: *Wait Until Your Dad Gets Home!*

T-Bone

My youngest son, T-Bone, was a senior in high school. He wrote a note to his dad on a Post-it® note and put it on the refrigerator door. I walked by the refrigerator and saw the note with two errors in it.

I said, "T-Bone, come in here. You have two errors on this note for your dad. You need to fix these."

T-Bone begrudgingly schlepped off to the kitchen table with a pencil in hand. He moaned and mumbled things under his breath. I gave him a new pad of Post-it® notes. He rewrote his note and slammed it onto the refrigerator.

I soon came back into the kitchen and stared at the note that still had one mistake. I said, "T-Bone, come in here. You still have a mistake on this note."

He said, "Mom, it doesn't have to be perfect."

"T-Bone, in this house, it does have to be perfect."

T-Bone labored away, and when he thought he had everything correct, he ripped off the Post-it® and slammed the paper onto the refrigerator door and said, "Nobody should ever have an English professor for a mother!"

That night, I went to teach my English class and told them the story about why I should never be my youngest son's mother. A student in my class said, "If you were my mother, I wouldn't even have to be here!"

High school photo of T-Bone and Jake.

A Budding Artist

What a blessing that I was able to be at the hospital on the day my granddaughter Leilani came into this world! I loved her before she was born and

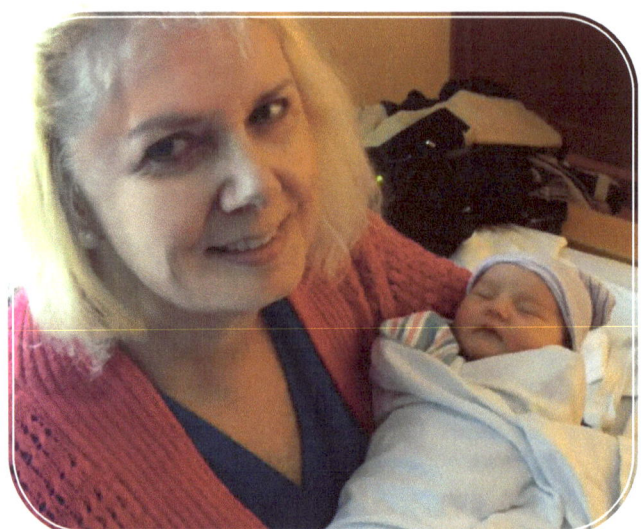

thrilled that she was in my arms only minutes after being born. I was there to hear her father sing to her and see the smiles on the faces of her parents.

I held Leilani in my arms only minutes after she was born.

At a young age Leilani began drawing. She especially likes to draw pictures of her family and animals. She includes these drawings on the special cards she makes for me. Leilani drew this picture of my service dog Charley in her note to me for Mother's Day. She was six years old when she made this drawing. Leilani even included the white tip on Charley's tail and the scar on his forehead. What a joy she is in my life.

A card from Leilani.

A Bedtime Story for Leilani

My granddaughter loves stories, especially true ones, like this one.

Once upon a time, Uncle Marty lived in the desert in New Mexico. One night he heard wings flapping in the bathroom vent. Uncle Marty thought the bird would figure out how to get out by morning, and so he went to bed. But in the morning the bird was still struggling to get out. It was time for Uncle Marty to put on his Superman cape and come to the bird's rescue.

Uncle Marty climbed onto the roof of his house and saw that the bird was at the bottom of a pipe that was about four inches wide and four feet long. Somehow the bird fell down this pipe, and there was no way the bird could fly out because he couldn't spread his wings. The sun was quickly heating up the roof. Uncle Marty was starting to sweat, and it was only seven o'clock in the morning. If he didn't get the bird out soon, the bird would die.

Being a clever man, Uncle Marty hauled the vacuum cleaner onto the roof. He hoped to use suction to pull the bird out. The vacuum machine roared into action. Uncle Marty put the tube down the pipe, and the bird moved out of the way. This went on for a few minutes, but the bird refused to go along with Uncle Marty's plan.

Uncle Marty then got his phone out of his pocket and called a roofer and asked him how he should cut a hole in the roof so the bird could fly out. Just as Uncle Marty was going to cut a hole in the roof, he got another idea.

Leaning over the pipe, he talked to the bird and said, "Okay, bird. I am going to throw you a rope, and you need to take it and climb out." Uncle Marty could feel the heat of the roof under his feet as he unplugged the cord to the vacuum and fed it down the pipe. Soon he felt a little weight on the cord, and it moved. In a couple of minutes, the bird and Uncle Marty were eye-to-eye. Then the bird spread his tired wings and flew to a nearby tree. There he sat until he recovered, and he sang a song as he looked at Uncle Marty.

Uncle Marty waved to the bird as it flew off, most likely to explain to his wife why he didn't come home last night. We heard that the bird's wife was mad and said, "Oh sure! You spent the night on a bathroom fan? Tell me another good story!"

Leilani

My husband and I were having lunch at a nice restaurant with our granddaughter, Leilani, and her parents—our youngest son and his wife.

Leilani is studying Spanish, and while we were waiting for our orders to arrive, I thought I would ask Leilani some questions in Spanish.

I asked her, "*¿Cómo estás?*" "How are you?"

She said, "*Bien.*" "Good."

"*¿Cómo te llamas?*" "What's your name?"

"Leilani."

I said, "*¿Cuántos años tienes?*" "How old are you?"

She said, "*Tengo siete años.*" "I'm seven years old."

I could tell she was getting tired of answering questions, but she was ready for my next question as she fiddled with her fork.

Leilani wearing my husband's hat and pearls that I gifted to her.

"*¿Cuál es tu restaurante favorito?*" "What is your favorite restaurant?"

She rolled her eyes and said, "*Este restaurante. . . . Hasta luego, Abuela!*" "This restaurant. . . . See you later, Grandma!"

She makes me laugh!

Running for the Arizona Senate

I challenged my youngest son, T-Bone, his wife Angie, and our grand-daughter, Leilani, to guess what our big news was at lunch at a favorite restaurant. After being seated and placing our orders, my husband and I asked for their guess.

Their guess? My daughter-in-law said, "Mom, you're pregnant!"

"No," I said, "I'm running for the Arizona Senate seat in Legislative District 13."

My son and daughter-in-law were stunned and silent. Leilani broke the silence and said, "Grandma, what is a senator?" She was seven years old.

Her mother said, "Senators make laws."

My political road sign.

Leilani did not seem happy about this turn of events. She would rather have a new baby in the family. Or perhaps she already had enough laws in her life: when to go to bed, what dessert she could have, schoolwork, and chores.

The lunch conversation soon turned to the usual topics as we enjoyed our family time together, but Leilani was unusually quiet as she listened to our conversations and drew some cartoon characters on her paper as we waited for our orders. My service dog Charley was with us, of course.

Our food was delicious, and we had dessert. Chocolate ice cream for me. After lunch we all walked out to the parking lot. I held Charley's leash in my left hand, and Leilani took my right hand as she said, "So Grandma, what law would you pass first as a senator?" She looked serious and stopped walking as she turned toward me and waited for my answer.

I looked at her beautiful and sweet face as I said, "The first law I would pass is a law that says, 'No one can eat chocolate ice cream except on Saturday and Sunday.'"

She knitted her brow as she said, "Grandma, not even you would like that law!"

Chocolate ice cream is safe in Arizona. I lost to the incumbent senator by 7,000 votes out of 114,000 votes.

Leilani's drawing of Charley on a card for me.

Paws

These are the paws that walked into my life and began to heal my heart after the loss of my dog, Karl.

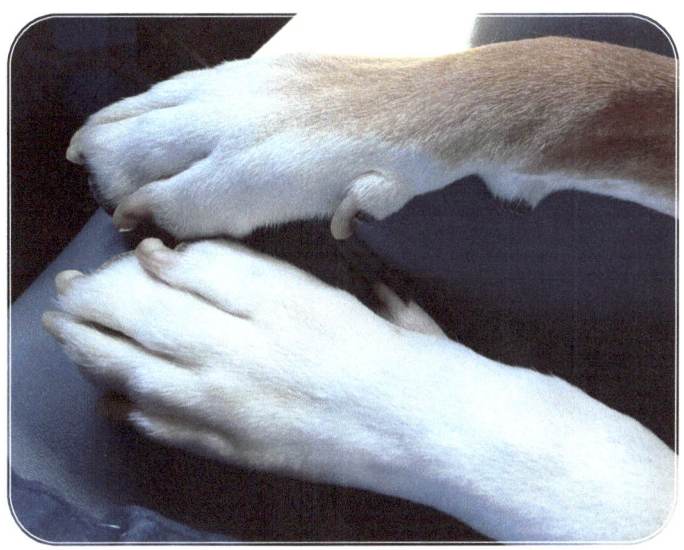

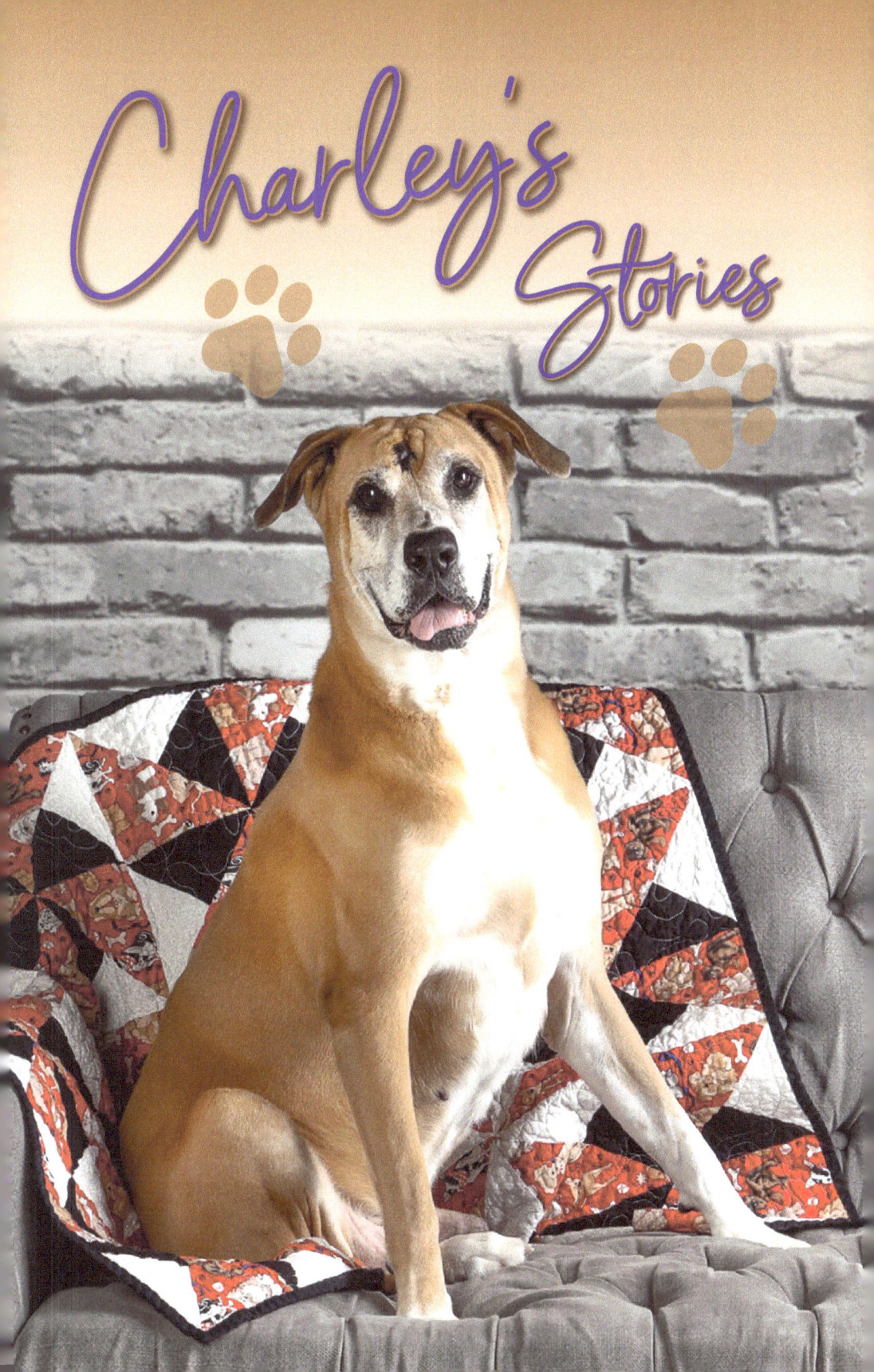

A New Life for Charley

December 30, 2021. Charley here: Breakfast is being served at the Maricopa County Animal Care and Control shelter where there are about five hundred dogs. There are about fifty dogs in my wing, all barking and excited. I'm not barking, and no one looks at me.

Last December a kind woman named Brittie found me wandering in a park, and her husband Jesse brought me to the shelter. One thousand animals are brought here every month. I saw a doctor when I first came in, and I got a lot of shots, and a microchip put into my neck. After that, I was put into a small kennel, about five-feet by five-feet, but it did have a doorway so I could go outside into a small space. Even though there are a lot of dogs around me, and the caretakers are kind and loving, I feel alone.

I'm about nine years old. That's old for a dog. I'm a big dog, too, and I have a large scar on my forehead. No one here knows what happened to me, but I remember. A horse kicked me! My life hasn't been an easy one.

My initial photo taken at the homeless shelter.

February 21, 2022. Last night, a chocolate-colored dog with golden eyes walked into my dream. He said, "Hey Charley, of all the dogs in all the towns in all the world, you will be chosen to go to a special forever home. Your hard life is over, and all will be right with the world.

Karl with the golden eyes.

"A man and a woman will come here tomorrow and take you to their home filled with love and peace. You will want for nothing and never be yelled at or hit. You'll love the food. The attention and love will fill your heart with happiness.

"But you should know a few things first. The woman likes to quilt and play the piano. When she quilts, your duty is to keep her company. When she plays the piano, go sit by her. You will enjoy hearing her music and watching her hands. The man likes to read and watch the news.

"Another thing you need to know is that you will be going for car rides, wearing a harness attached to a seat belt. You'll get used to it.

"Also, you will have a lot of aunties and uncles—too numerous to mention. They will all love you. One of them, Uncle Marty, will take care of you when the man and woman leave town. Going to his house will be fun, and the food is good there, too.

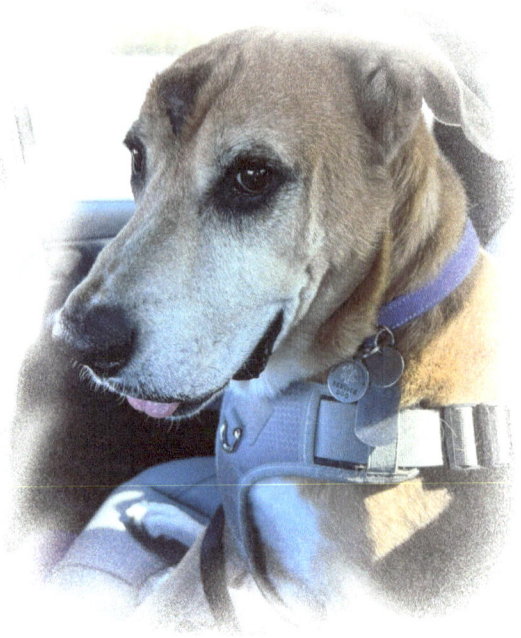

"Finally, you need to know there has been a problem at this house ever since I passed over the rainbow bridge. The woman has been crying a lot! The man tries to comfort her by hugging her tight and telling her how much he loves her, and she stops crying only to start again an hour later. The man says fixing her broken heart is above his pay grade. However, it's not above your pay grade, which is why I have chosen you. Your job is to fix her broken heart. Look into her eyes with all the love you have in your heart, and all will be right with the world.

"I'll be watching over you."

February 22, 2022. I thought and wondered about my dream all morning. Then this afternoon a caretaker came to my kennel and put a leash on me. I thought we were going for a walk, but she said, "Okay, Charley, this is your chance to have a nice home. There is a man and a woman who want to meet you."

My caretaker has been worried about me because the county can't keep dogs for a long time, and few people want large dogs like me. I weigh sixty-five pounds, but I should weigh about eighty-five pounds. That's small for a Great Dane, but no one would call me a small dog. And people don't want nine-year-old dogs like me, either. And then I have a big scar on my forehead and some smaller scars on my head and body, as well as large carbuncles on my elbows from living on cement. My caretaker says I'm handsome, but it's clear I've had a hard life.

My caretaker opened the gate to a grassy compound, and I saw the woman who was in my dream! As soon as she saw me twenty feet away, her face lit up with a smile. She turned to the man and said, "I love his face."

I continued to walk toward her, and when I was right in front of her, I looked into her eyes—just like the chocolate-colored dog told me to do.

The woman said to the man, "I want this dog." She reached out and gently stroked my face and ears. She didn't care about the scar on my face, and she didn't care that I was an older dog.

The man looked at the woman, looked at me, and said, "Sweetheart, are you sure? He's a big dog. Much bigger than Karl." The man was not sure if he wanted to take me home. I kept looking at the woman.

Again, she said to the man, "I want this dog."

He said, "But are you sure?" The woman just stared back at the man and kept petting my face.

He said, "Okay, let's take him home. Happy wife, happy life."

The woman was in love with me as soon as she saw my face. I went over to the man, and he touched my face with a gentleness I had never felt before. Now the man was in love with me, too. That took five minutes.

My caretaker who brought me into the compound broke out in a big smile. She said, "He is such a sweet dog. You will love him. We call him 'The Gentle Giant.'" She was bursting with happiness for me as she led me away to get me ready for my forever home.

As the man and woman stepped up to the county clerk's window, the man repeated his earlier concern, "Sweetheart, he's a very big dog."

She said, "I don't care. I want him." They signed a lot of paperwork, and I was adopted under my new mommy's family name. The county gave me a special leash and collar with a shiny new tag with a number on it. The clerk changed all the information that went with my microchip. I had a new name, Charley Winters, and a new home address.

I was waiting outside with two people from the kennel when my new daddy pulled their car up next to me. Mommy was already in the back seat, but I was afraid of the car. I had seen how dangerous they could be while I was living on my own. Couldn't we just walk to my new home?

It took four people to get me into that car! My new mommy stayed in the back seat with me on the ride home.

This is a picture of me on the way to my forever home. I put my head and paw on my new mommy's lap. She petted and talked to me in a soothing voice all the way home.

I'm on my way to my forever home.

Next to my mommy in the scary car.

My First Night in My New Home

February 22, 2022 (continued). The ride to my new home was scary, and then the car stopped. It took both Mommy and Daddy to get me out of the car. They took me into a big house. I was still scared.

Daddy put a big bowl of water in the kitchen on a mat. I drank a lot of water, and then he took me out to a beautiful backyard. When I saw the yard, I thought, Wowzah! Is this all mine?!

Wowzah! My new backyard.

I'm looking forward to dinner tonight. Daddy said it's Angus beef night and that I need to put on some weight. I'm okay with that! Mommy is going to be counting my calories, and I get to see my new doctor on Saturday. I have all my shots, so I think this will be a meet-and-greet kind of thing. I bet the doctor will be so happy to see me because he knows my new mommy has been crying a lot.

When I came back into the house, Mommy fixed my dinner. She said, "I'll fix you a better dinner tomorrow, Charley."

She pointed out to Daddy where my ribs and spine were showing, and when Daddy saw what Mommy was fixing for me, he said, "That dinner won't last long."

My dinner was two Angus beef patties with gravy and some kibble that the shelter gave to Daddy for me. Dinner was delicious!

Later that evening, Daddy took me into a bedroom and said, "Here's your bed, Charley."

I stepped onto my bed, and it was soft. That's when I saw the quilt on Mommy's and Daddy's bed. I went over to the quilt and tried to pull it off. Mommy said, "No, Charley. This quilt is not for you."

My First Day in My New Home

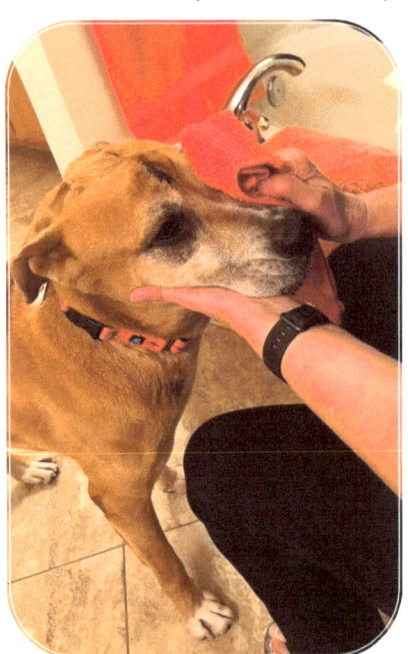

*Mommy washing my face
for the first time.*

February 23, 2022. I'm sitting here by Mommy's feet and resting. I made it through my first night, but I didn't get much sleep. I have a big soft bed in their bedroom. I'm an outside dog, so this was new for me.

Today Mommy measured me for a seat belt harness to wear in the car. And I discovered a big box of toys! Daddy said they were all mine. I liked the lamb and walked with it around the house. I'm gentle with squeaky toys, so I didn't bite down hard enough for it to make any noise.

Here's how my day started: Mommy washed my eyes and face with warm water on a washcloth, combed my fur, and put a silicone gel on the scar on my forehead to soften it. The gel was soothing and stopped that "pulling" sensation.

Then Daddy gave me three cups of kibble for breakfast. I ate about a cup of it. I'm holding out for dinner, which is going to be another Angus beef and gravy night. Mommy said she would go to the store to get me better food and not give me any more kibble.

But here's the best part. I figured out how to say, "I want to go outside." All I do is ruffle the curtain on the door to the backyard! When they see me do that, I get to go outside. They are so smart!

This grass is nice!

And then here's the other good part. This is a picture of me by Mommy's feet while she is cutting fabric for her quilt on her cutting table. She is careful not to step on me, and she also stops to give me lots of petting. I like to be close to her.

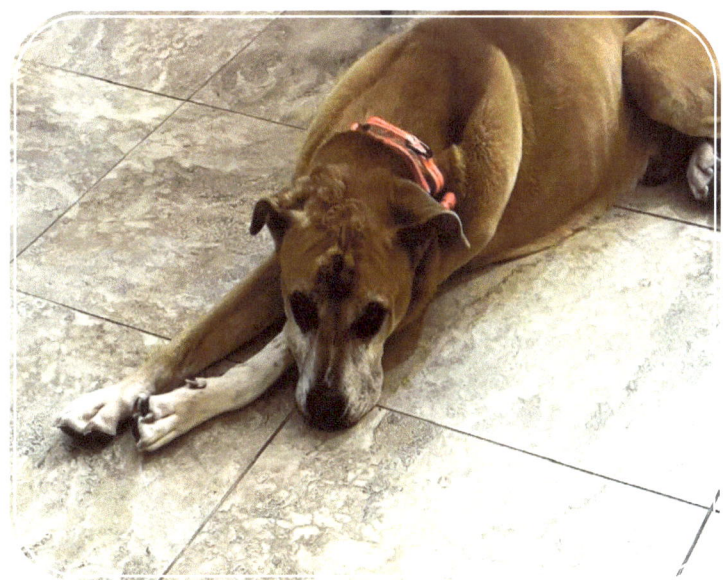

Keeping Mommy company while she quilts.

Here is a picture of Mommy's sewing machine. I keep hoping she'll share some of her yummy-smelling sewing supplies with me, but she keeps my treats in a different room.

I'm not sure what to think about Mommy washing my face and wiping my eyes with warm water on a soft cloth. I like it, but I don't get it. I stand really still for Mommy.

Several times a day I go out to the backyard. Sometimes Daddy comes outside with me, and I follow him around the yard. Hmmm . . . Where is he going? Is he lost?

These are sewing supplies?

Bad Dream

February 23, 2022 (continued). I had a bad dream in the middle of the night. I cried and howled. Daddy got up with me. He asked, "What's the matter, Charley? You are having a bad dream. Let's go outside." The air was warm, and when I looked at the sky, there were a lot of stars. When Daddy took me back into the bedroom, I glanced again at the quilt. I really wanted a quilt for my bed, too, but I knew that quilt was not for me.

The next day, I took a lap quilt off the couch. Mommy said, "This quilt is not for you." Understood. But what *could* I have?

The "Look"

February 26, 2022. I was a good boy at my doctor's office today. The doctor said I'm about nine-years old, and I tested negative for heartworm. My doctor was happy to meet me, and he said I was a calm boy.

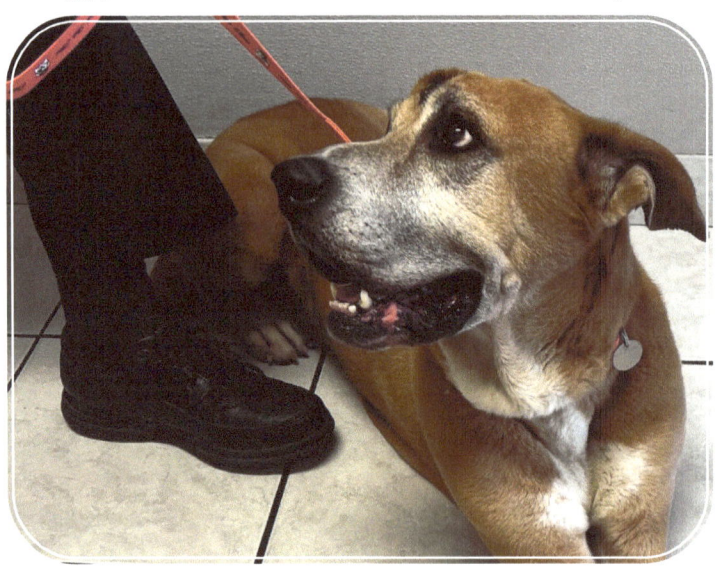

Daddy will protect me at the doctor's office.

Mommy told my new doctor that since I have come into her life, she has stopped crying. My doctor said, "Happy wife, happy life." I'm happy, too! As my doctor was leaving the room, he gave us all a big smile and then looked at my mommy, patted her shoulder, and said, "No more crying." He was happy for all of us.

At lunch Mommy told Daddy, "If you could look at me the way Charley looks at me, your life would be a whole lot different."

He said, "You mean I could have almost anything I want?"

Mommy said, "Not almost anything. You could have anything, anytime."

Daddy said he's going to have to watch me carefully and copy my look! Good luck, Daddy.

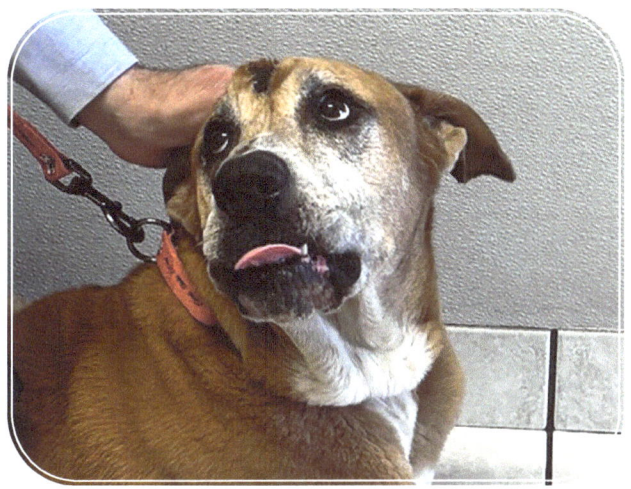

Daddy knows how to comfort me when I'm scared.

Welcome

This is my new home?!

March 1, 2022. I'm feeling very welcomed into this family of many aunties, uncles, and cousins. After Mommy posted my picture on my first day in my new home, all my new aunties and uncles were so happy they kept Mommy busy all day with their welcome messages for me.

And today I received a pile of gifts from Auntie Mil, Uncle Andre, Cousin Keela, and Cousin Magnum, Auntie Mary, Uncle Terry, and cousin Gabby. Wowzah!

I love all of my new Aunties and Uncles!

I love all of my new

Such GREAT news, Sharon!!! Seeing Charley's face I can see why it was love at first sight for you! ENJOY this bee-YOO-tee-full guy!!! *XOXO XOXO XOXO XOXO XOXO.* ~ Uncle Robert

What a lucky dog. Auntie Anita

Do you have a big heart or what, Sharon? Is this your new baby, Charley? Hurry, I need a full size photo of this big guy. ~ Auntie Alice

Oh, he looks sweeeeeet! Can't wait to see many new pics of Charley! ~ Auntie Tina

Hi Charley! Your sad eyes will soon relax because you now have a great Mom and Dad! Just wait till you have dinner . . . oh boy! Everyone sends their love. ❤️Auntie Elizabeth

Oh SHARON, I'M SO HAPPY for you, your Hubby and CHARLEY!! KARL IS SO PROUD OF YOU, TOO . . . MORE PICTURES PLEASE! ~ Auntie Barb

Your new mom and dad are lucky to have found you!! Welcome to the family! 💕💕💕Auntie Kerry

❤️ 👍 😎 Uncle Gerald

Happy for you and Charley! Way-to-go! ~ Uncle Jim

Lucky Charley!!! I see love all around. ❤️Auntie Tami

Charley, you are going to the best home. You will get good food and lots of love. Gabby was a rescue and she says welcome to the family. ❤️🐶Auntie Mary, Uncle Terry, and Gabby

Great news. Love that face! So glad you found him. Welcome to the family, Charley! ~ Auntie Hazel

Breaks my heart but now he will be happy. ~ Auntie Krissy

Awwwwwww 🥰 what sweet eyes. Sounds like this poor baby had a rough time in his previous home. ☹️Auntie Janis

That makes me very happy. Hugs. Thank you for naming him after me. ~ Uncle Chuck

Aunties and Uncles!

Precious! Definitely huggable. 💙Auntie Julianne

Sharon, be prepared to double the menu . . . LOL. Welcome to the family, Charley!! ~ Auntie Myra

Welcome to your forever home! We can't wait to hear more from you! ~ Auntie Yvonne

You can always tell a good dog by its eyes, very lucky dog. So much fun ahead for all of you. ❤️Auntie Cookie

The heartache of losing a pet is balanced by the need and capacity to love another one. Karl gets that, and is happy for you. ❤️Auntie Gloria

It'll probably take a month before you'll need to go on a diet (😛), but the journey will be fulfilling and filled with love (not to mention delicious)! Welcome! ~ Uncle Terry

He is so sweet. We have a Mastiff mix, also. She's 14 now. After he gets some good food in him, if he's like my dog, he will be like the Energizer Bunny! ~ Auntie Myranette

Oh those eyes. Such a lucky guy to have you. He will certainly receive loads of love and special food for sure. Won't be able to see those ribs for long! 💙 👏 ~ Auntie Bobbi

So awesome. This guy is deserving of everything we can give!! ~ Auntie Sue

That's awesome! Congratulations! ❤️ So happy he has his forever loving home, and the best mommy and daddy. ~ Auntie Lynn

All of you are sooooooo lucky. Rescues are the best. On my 23rd. Big congratulations. ~ Auntie Pamela

Awwww, what a great adoption! ~ Auntie Laura

Thank you!

Oopsie! Sorry, Daddy

March 1, 2022 (continued). I've been having a great time with all my doggy toys. I take toys with me everywhere I go in the house, when I go outside, and for sure, when I go to bed. Most of my toys squeak, which I love, especially since I figured out how to gently squeeze them with my mouth to make that fun-sounding noise. Sometimes I put my toys in pairs.

I follow Mommy around the house, so I want toys in every room. This is a picture of me in Mommy's workroom with one of my toys.

Last night I took two toys to bed with me like I always do. And if Mommy or Daddy get up in the middle of the night, I wake up because I only sleep with one eye closed. I know it is my job to keep an eye out for them. When they are both safely back in bed, I go back to sleep. I can even snore with one watchful eye open.

This is my frog toy I like to carry around.

Last night I thought Mommy was going to get up, and I lifted my head to watch her. As I shifted in bed, I accidentally slammed my heavy paw on one of my squeaky toys. Daddy woke up and said, "Did you hear that whistle? What was that?!"

Oopsie. Sorry, Daddy!

Early Days

March 3, 2022. My life in my new home hasn't always been about eating and sleeping and playing with new toys. Mommy and Daddy also began teaching me basic obedience commands using a thing that makes a clicking noise. I taught them that I was a slow learner, and I needed more treats than most dogs. It worked!

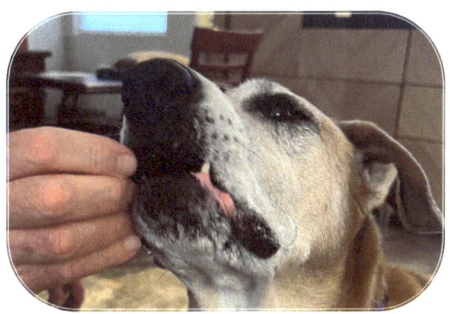

Daddy gives me lots of treats.

Mommy hired a dog trainer and guess who has homework?! Not me! Bwahahaha! All I need to do is eat treats when I hear a clicking noise. Karl's favorite cheese was Provolone cheese. So now I get to eat Provolone cheese. Mommy presses the clicker and then gives me a piece of cheese. Her homework was to do that fifteen times. Then it was Daddy's turn to use the clicker, and I ate fifteen more little pieces of cheese. I think they need to do more homework tomorrow and the day after that and the day after that . . .

Mommy says it's clicker training. Okay. Just keep the cheese coming.

Dog Tags

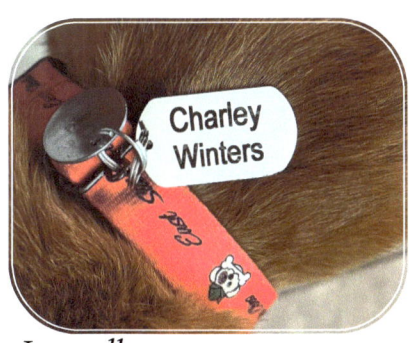

I proudly wear my new name.

March 5, 2022. Mommy said that when she and Daddy adopted me that it's a legal thing, and I was given a new name, which was registered with the State of Arizona. That's the round tag on my collar that I received before I left the custody of the county. And yesterday a dog tag came in the mail. I really like it. It has my legal name on one side and on the other side it says "Mommy" and her phone number and "Daddy" and his phone number. The county put the orange collar on me along with the round tag before I could leave with my new parents. My tags make a nice noise when I walk. They play a jingle: "I'm a happy boy . . . I'm a happy boy . . ."

Toys

March 5, 2022 (continued). Auntie Mary and Uncle Terry, thank you for the new toys! I love them. I'm taking these to bed with me tonight. They are all my favorites.

I placed some of my toys in a row and then in a "four" pattern. Mommy says I played checkers in a former life.

Toys from Auntie Mary and Uncle Terry.

Just keeping my toys organized.

New Bed

March 5, 2022 (continued). Holy moly! Mommy and Daddy got a nice big orthopedic bed for me. My sleep time is wonderful with this new bed.

My new orthopedic bed.

Things have been going well for me. Mommy has been putting scar gel on the scar on my forehead, and the swelling is going down. I get my face and eyes washed, and Mommy has been putting "ear wash" in my ears every day. It tickles.

And there is plenty of food for me because now I can eat what I want and leave the rest for later if I'm hungry. I used to grab a bite of food and run. I don't have to do that anymore. Daddy says I'm still skinny, and my doctor wants me to put on a little weight. I've gone from sixty-five pounds to sixty-seven, but I'm still skinny.

There's food for me when I want to eat, and I'm getting lots of attention. All is right with the world.

The Washcloth

March 8, 2022. I've been taking Daddy's washcloth and dropping it on the bathroom floor in front of Mommy's sink for three nights in a row. Mommy can't take a hint. So last night, when Daddy said, "Okay Charley, it's time to go to bed," I just gave him a pleading look and didn't move toward my nice bed. Daddy was puzzled because I usually like going to bed.

Finally, Mommy told Daddy, "Charley keeps dropping your washcloth

on the bathroom floor by my sink."

Daddy said, "Oh! That's why he won't go to bed. He wants his face washed."

Mommy looked at Daddy like he had a screw loose. She said, "Really? How do you know?"

Daddy said he just knows. So, Mommy washed my face, and I sighed with contentment. That warm wet soft cloth felt so good! After my face was washed, I went right over to my bed.

*I need my face washed before
I can sleep.*

Daddy had an I-told-you-so look on his face, but he kept that to himself. He wasn't sure there was room for the two of us on my nice bed.

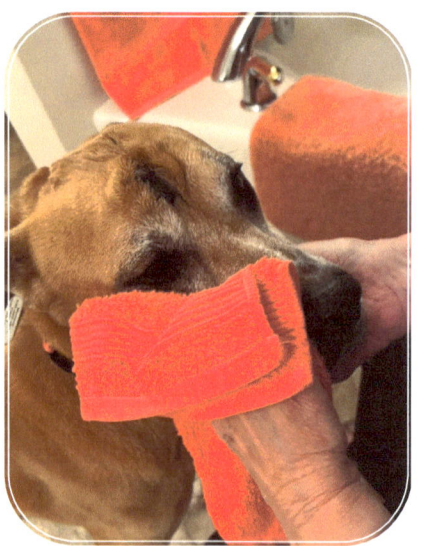

Feels so good!

Dropping Hints

March 11, 2022. I've been dropping hints for days that I need my own blanket. I took bath towels, two of Mommy's sweaters, hand towels, washcloths, dish towels, bathmats . . . whatever I could find. Mommy would always take them away from me and say, "This is not for you, Charley."

I even tried to take the big quilt off Mommy and Daddy's bed, but it was tucked in at the bottom. I really wanted a quilt for my bed, too!

Mommy told Daddy, "Charley needs a blanket."

Daddy said, "No, he doesn't."

"Yes I do, Daddy." I took the small quilt off Mommy's side of the bed and brought it into the living room.

Mommy told Daddy again, "Charley needs a blanket."

Daddy said, "No, he doesn't."

Mommy rolled her eyes. I wish I could do that. Mommy called Uncle Marty and said, "Charley needs a blanket. Do you have one you could give Charley?"

All is right with the world.

Uncle Marty loves me.

Uncle Marty said, "Sure! I'll wash one for him and bring it over."

I was so excited when the doorbell rang. "Uncle Marty! Uncle Marty!" He laid a beautifully hand-made crocheted afghan on the living room area rug for me. I snuggled into it, and it was so soft and wonderful, I took a little nap.

Last night Mommy moved the afghan to my bed for me. I heard Daddy say to Mommy, "You were right!"

Mommy whispered in my ear as she kissed the top of my head goodnight, "As usual . . ."

Thank you for the afghan, Uncle Marty!

Doctor's Report

March 17, 2022. I was a good boy at my doctor's office today. I weighed sixty-five pounds before I was adopted. Today I weighed 73.2 pounds. My doctor said that's a good weight for me, and he was happy to see that my ribs are not showing like they were.

He also said I must have had a hard life before, and he's happy for me that I have a good home now.

I opened up a scar on my side by scratching it, and the nurse used a laser-like treatment on my wound. It's not itchy now, and it should be healed in a few days with this special treatment.

I was a good boy when the nurse was cutting my nails.

AND no more ear wash because there's no more ear wax in my ears. My ears are nice and clean. But I think I still need my face and eyes washed twice a day. He didn't say to stop that!

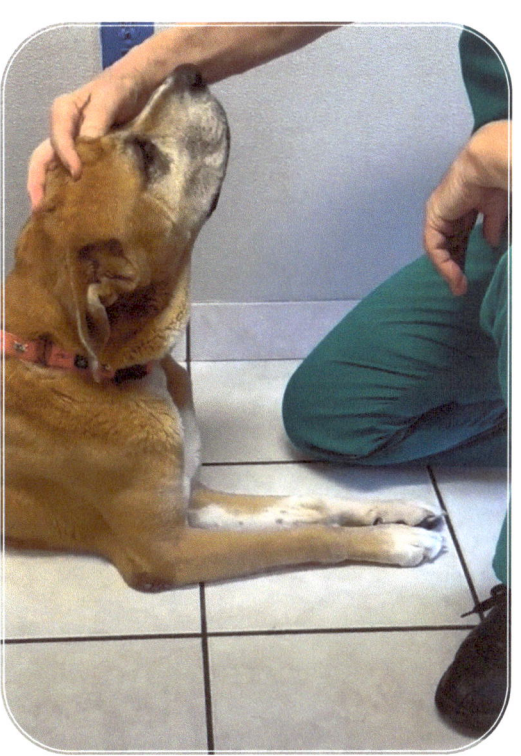

Dr. Benish is kind to me.

Hot Air Balloon

March 19, 2022. I love my new backyard, but this morning I saw a large hot air balloon with some people in it. I didn't want the noisy balloon to land in my new yard, so I barked at it until it went away. The nerve of that balloon to threaten our neighborhood!

Mommy said, "Charley, you saved the whole neighborhood from that hot air balloon!"

I was so proud and happy, I wagged my tail. I love being a good boy.

Charley the Service Dog

My first service dog vest!

April 2, 2022. Today there was a knock on the door and a strong tall man was at the door. When he came into the house, he said hello to me, and Mommy put my leash on my collar as she said, "Today you are going to go with this nice man who is going to train you to be my service dog."

He took my leash and took me to the sidewalk. No! I didn't want to leave my home! I pulled against the leash and tried to get back into the house. "No, Daddy! No, Mommy! Don't let him take me away!" He kept using words like: *Let's go, Yes, Sit, Stay, Come, Good boy.* Finally he said, "Let's go home." He gave me a lot of treats! I liked that part, and I was even happier when he brought me back home.

School was a lot of work for me! This went on for several months with him coming to my house and taking me to the sidewalk. My trainer was kind. His treats were good. He taught me to walk on Mommy's left side and walk at her pace. He taught me to stop if she stops because she might need to touch the handle on my vest to keep her balance. And he taught me to help Mommy up curbs by putting my front feet on the sidewalk while she touches my vest handle and puts her feet onto the sidewalk. He also taught me to behave in public places like a restaurant—but I was a natural at that because I'm such a good boy. When he took me to a restaurant with my parents, he ordered a bowl of whipped cream for me!

After many training sessions my teacher said, "Charley, you have worked hard and earned a special vest. Let's put your vest on and take you back to your house." The vest said: SERVICE DOG. Now I was official!

When my teacher rang the doorbell, Daddy answered the door and yelled out to my mommy, "Charley is here, and he's wearing a vest!" Daddy petted my face and said, "Charley, we are so proud of you! Now you are Mommy's service dog."

Mommy came to the door and held my face in her hands. She kissed my forehead as she said, "We love you, Charley. You are such a good boy. And now you can always be with me."

I was ready for my work, and I love the thought of being with Mommy wherever she goes.

When I Bark, Dogs Listen

April 3, 2022. This morning, all the neighborhood dogs were barking, and Daddy said, "Charley, what do you have to say to all of those barking dogs?"

I went outside and gave out one big, deep, and loud WOOF! All of the dogs went silent. Daddy laughed and said, "Good boy, Charley. You told them you are the boss of the neighborhood!"

I'm Charley Winters!

Big Bark

April 8, 2022. I've got a bounce in my step and a smile on my face. I was just letting the neighborhood dogs know I'm a big boy with a big bark. I love everybody.

I'm a happy boy!

Mommy Has a Large Vocabulary

April 11, 2022. Mommy always rides in the back seat of the car with me. Even though I have a seat belt on, I'm five feet long from the tip of my nose to the end of my butt, and if I fly forward into the front seat in an accident, Mommy says I could get hurt. So, she hangs onto the collar of my vest as I sit or lie with my head next to her leg. She loves me and wants to keep me safe.

I love riding in the car now. However, today we were almost in a bad car accident on the freeway. Daddy was swerving right and left then right and left, and Mommy was saying words I never heard before. Mommy had a grip on my harness, and she kept me safe. I didn't know Mommy was that strong. I didn't know she had such a large vocabulary, either!

Spa Day

April 12, 2022. I rode in the car again this morning and nothing bad happened. Daddy and Mommy said I was going to get a bath. Daddy pulled into a parking spot and Mommy and Daddy talked to this nice woman, Annie, who led me away.

She gave me a nice warm bath with some good-smelling soap and trimmed my nails. That was all okay until she put me in a large kennel with a blower with warm air to dry my fur. That's when I got worried that I would

I like to be right next to my mommy.

never see my parents again. And there were a lot of dogs there just like at the county kennels.

But then Annie took me out of the kennel, put my harness for car rides back on me, and hooked my leash to my collar. She said, "Your mommy and daddy are here." She put a pretty scarf around my neck, too.

Yay! When Annie walked me out the door, there they were! Annie said, "Charley was such a good boy getting his bath and nails trimmed."

Daddy buckled me into my seat belt while Mommy paid Annie. Mommy got in the back seat with me, and I was soon back to my forever home.

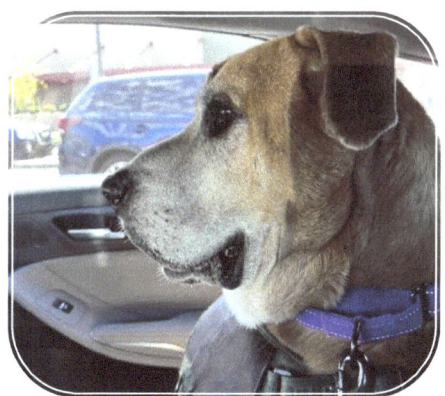

I sit like a person in the car sometimes.

Annie gave me a new bandana.

A Crime

May 14, 2022. Mommy committed a crime. My dinner tonight was cooked carrots with butter, plain Greek yogurt, and 9.5 ounces of *sous vide* cooked meat: chicken thigh meat, pork loin, and ground beef.

I couldn't believe she did this. She cooked my carrots, put butter on the carrots, and when the butter melted, she poured the melted butter in the TRASH! That's a crime! Noooooo! Dinner was good anyway.

DNA Test Results

May 16, 2022. My DNA test came back, and it says I'm half Boxer. Mommy says I look more like a Great Dane, but since Boxers were bred from Great Danes and other breeds, that DNA test may not be fully accurate. Uncle Chuck said that compared to a Boxer, I'm bigger with longer legs, and I have a long snout. He said he was skeptical of that test. Mommy agreed and said I even have a Great Dane tail. My other half includes German Shepherd, Husky, and other breeds I never heard of.

I'm okay being part German Shepherd, since I am smart and loyal. And I can sure howl like a Husky! But what breed I am makes no difference to me, so long as I can love and help Mommy.

I can howl like a Husky!

Bigger Bed, Please

May 27, 2022. The afghan Uncle Marty gave me is cozy, and I love it. But now I need a bigger bed!

I need a bigger bed!

A New Quilt

June 27, 2022. At bedtime, Mommy washed my face, I ate my treats, and I went to my bed. Mommy left the room, and Daddy looked toward the door. Mommy came in with a quilt, and I sat up in my bed. Mommy and Daddy each held a corner of the quilt so I could see it. Daddy said, "Mommy made this quilt, and this quilt is for you, Charley!"

I went over to the quilt. Wowzah! This quilt was for me!

Daddy put the quilt on my bed. I stepped onto my bed and snuggled into the quilt. It was so soft! As I fell asleep, I knew for sure that all was right with the world.

I never again took another quilt, towel, or bath mat to my bed. I'm such a good boy, and I had a quilt that was made just for me.

My very own quilt.

Blue Cone Fashion

July 16, 2022. Yesterday Mommy and Daddy took me to the emergency room because my left front paw hurt. I was limping, and I didn't want that sore paw to touch the ground. I was nervous!

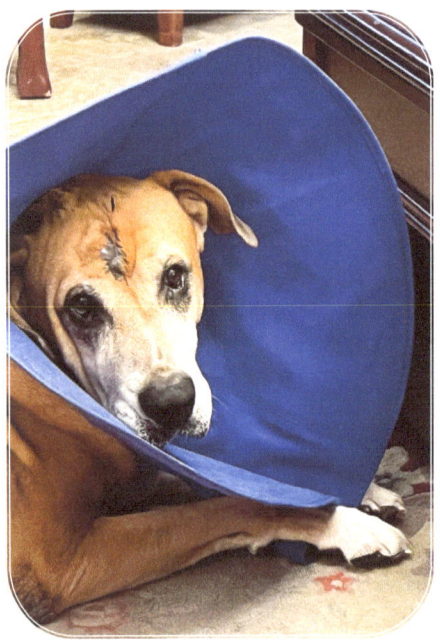

The cone!

The doctor said my paw was infected. I got a blood test to check my kidneys to see if I can take a steroid. I was also tested for Valley Fever because it's common in Arizona. The doctor sent me home with antibiotics to take for ten days. He also gave me a big cone and said I have to wear it! That did not make me happy, and I'm still limping.

But the pills are helping, and I'm getting used to my floppy hat. At least, I was able to sleep with the blue cone on, and Mommy said I'm still handsome, so all is right with the world.

It's a hat!

The Scale Tells a Tale

July 17, 2022. The first thing that happened at the emergency room yesterday was not easy with a sore paw. I had to step up and stand on a big scale. When I was first brought to my new home, I weighed sixty-five pounds, and my ribs and spine were showing. Now I'm eighty-five pounds. But the doctor said I looked good. Whew! No diets for me!

But then the doctor asked Mommy what she feeds me. Uh oh! (Why do doctors always ask that question?!) She said dinner is cooked carrots or green beans, a cup of Greek yogurt, and 9.5 ounces of meat: chicken thigh, pork loin, and Angus beef with twenty percent fat. Then, she listed all the supplements she gives me to make sure I stay healthy. Plus I get beef jerky and cod fish skins every day—of course!

The doctor said to put me on leaner meats.

So today Mommy and Daddy brought home sixteen pounds of meat: center cut pork loin, lean ground beef with only twelve percent fat, and chicken breasts. She mixed the meats together and then divided them up into 9.5-ounce packages. I have enough meat for twenty-eight days. All the packages were cooked in the *sous vide* cooker in Food Saver bags. Most of the bags went into the freezer for my future dinners.

This food is all for me.

I tell you what! I had to smell that meat cooking ALL day. At dinnertime tonight, I supervised Mommy making my dinner, and she gave me one of those packages of cooked meat. I look forward to my dinners every day! All is right with the world.

*Chicken, pork loin, and
lean ground beef for my dinner.*

Sleeping?

July 25, 2022. I'm always by my mommy because she needs me. I may look like I'm sleeping, but I'm not. I have one eye open. If Mommy gets up from her chair, I'm awake and I follow her—because she needs me to be with her wherever she goes. My favorite time is dinnertime. I'll be in the kitchen while she fixes my dinner.

I can sleep with one eye open.

My favorite place—by Mommy.

The Secret to My Scar

September 2, 2022. Mommy and Daddy finally found out how I got that scar on my forehead. When I went to my doctor's office today for a blood test, two veterinarian technicians came in, and one of them had something important to share.

She said, "I've been meaning to tell you that I first met Charley when I worked at another clinic, and Charley was about three years old.

"He came into the clinic with a terrible head wound from being kicked by a horse. We were surprised he was alive, and he was so good when we were putting in stitches. We were grateful he didn't have any brain damage. He was such a sweet boy, just like he is now."

Mommy said, "Whoever owned him before can't have him back."

Good! Because I want to stay with my mommy and daddy.

The technicians wanted to take me to another room to draw my blood, but Mommy said, "No, we should be with him." I was glad I wouldn't be by myself.

I was really good when the technician took my blood from my front leg. Daddy held me in his arms, and another technician held me in her arms, too. Mommy talked to me in a soothing voice and told me what a good boy I am. I was happy I got to stay with my parents. I can depend on them to protect me.

Captured in Crayon

November 7, 2022. I love Mommy's granddaughter, Leilani. Here is a drawing she made of me. She even included the scar on my forehead.

Leilani was five years old when she drew my portrait.

Braveheart

November 16, 2022. Daddy and I are the Great Protectors; Mommy said so. And tonight there was a crashing sound in the utility room, which is at the end of a long dark hallway. There's a door that goes into the utility room from the garage. We all heard that sound.

Mommy went into the kitchen because she thought the noise came from something falling off a counter. Daddy and I knew better. The sound came from the utility room. Daddy motioned for Mommy to stay where she was in the kitchen while Daddy and I silently sprang into action. Someone could be breaking into our house! We snuck down the dark hallway like Ninjas. I let Daddy lead the way. I told him, "I've got your back, Daddy!"

When Daddy and I got to the utility room, no one was there, or Mommy would have heard a horrible ruckus as we "took care of business" if you know what I mean. Between Daddy's readiness and my eighty-five pounds of fearlessness as Daddy's backup, someone would be sorry.

There was a laundry basket on the floor that hadn't been there before. Daddy said the vibrations of the dryer caused that plastic basket to fall off the dryer onto the floor. I sniffed it just to make sure no one but Mommy had touched it. It passed the sniff test, so all was right with the world. Good job, Daddy. You told that basket a thing or two.

Just call me Braveheart!

Charley at a Mensa Convention

Mommy, me, and my trainer Jordan at a Mensa convention.

November 27, 2022. Mommy took me to a Mensa convention, and she talked about the books she has published. It wasn't very exciting for me until I met another service dog. Wowzah! She was a beauty! She was a silver-gray Labradoodle. When she saw me, she said, "Hey, handsome! I see you're a working dog, too."

I said, "You're gorgeous! Yeah, I'm a working dog, too." As she passed by me, we touched noses. It was an exciting moment. We were both well behaved—no barking or whining or anything. Just some tail wags. The rest of it was downhill. I tried to get a little shut-eye.

One of my two trainers, Jordan, was there, too. He talked about my training and said, "In all my time of training dogs, I've never seen a dog who loved someone as much as Charley loves Sharon."

The Sniff Test

December 8, 2022. Not everyone knows this, but dogs can smell more than 10,000 times better than humans. Today we went to a seafood restaurant, and as soon as we walked in the door, the smells were delectable. And there was a guy wearing Bermuda shorts who was eating something I just had to sniff. He was about twenty feet away.

As we were walking to a table in the back where I could stretch out, I determined by quadrant projection that we were going to pass by him, and he was going to be on my left. I had one chance to get my sniff as we headed in his direction.

When I had my chance, I accidentally on purpose touched his warm leg with my wet and cold nose. Wowzah! He was eating fish with butter! As I took my sniff, Mr. Bermuda Shorts jumped. It was just a little sniff.

Daddy apologized. But who can blame me? It was 3:15 and I usually get my dinner at 3:00. My dinner of London broil, fresh blueberries, carrots, and Greek yogurt was being delayed. Besides that, it was just a little sniff, and I was starving!

Drawing Details

January 14, 2023. I really and truly love Leilani. Here is another drawing she made of me. She remembered the white on the end of my tail. And my four white paws.

Leilani's portrait of me when she was six years old.

Another Sore Paw

March 5, 2023. Mommy and Daddy had to take me to the emergency room again because I was limping. This time it's my right front paw. My heart and temperature are good, but the doctor thinks my paw is infected.

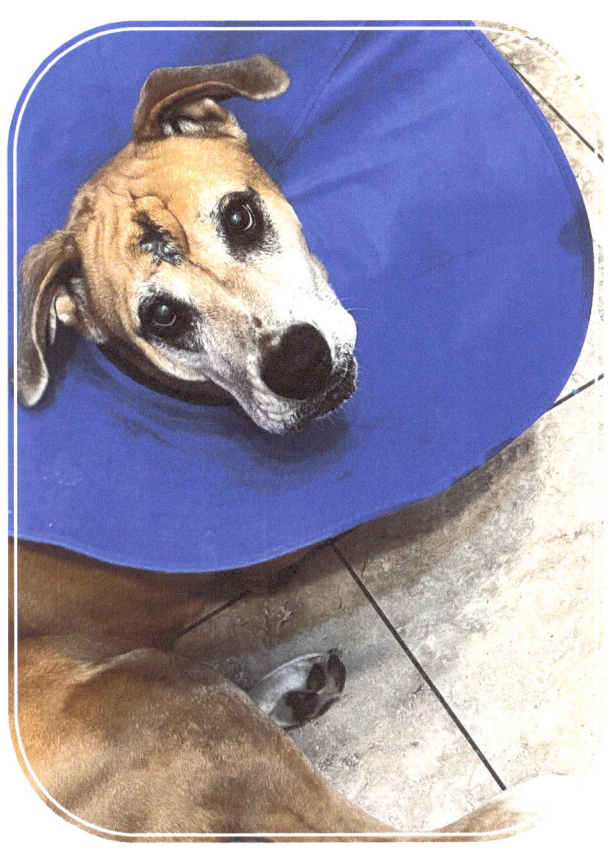

He gave me an allergy shot, and antibiotics to take. Mommy wraps my pills in something delicious, so I gulp them right down. I also have to wear . . . the CONE! I know I will feel better soon. The doctor said I can't work for awhile, so Mommy and Daddy put me on paid sick leave.

Good thing I'm on sick leave. Now I don't have to be seen in public wearing this ridiculous hat.

Okay Now

March 12, 2023. I'm okay now to be Mommy's service dog again because my paw is healed, and I'm not limping anymore. We went to lunch today with Uncle Marty, and when we were all leaving, a man passed by me and said, "Hey, big man! Hello!" I wagged my tail politely, but didn't he realize I was actually a big dog?

Tragedy

March 13, 2023. My Uncle Marty died tonight. I feel like howling. Mommy and Daddy took me to the hospital with them. A doctor and nurse took the three of us to a small room with cushioned chairs. That's when the doctor said, "We did everything we could to save him." I was at Mommy's feet as she cried, and Daddy took Mommy's hand.

Celebration of Life

April 17, 2023. Yesterday was Uncle Marty's celebration of life. Leilani was there, of course, with her dad and mom, T-Bone and Angie. There were over twenty people at Marty's house. Someone made a lot of food, although none of it was for me, and someone else made a video showing pictures of Uncle Marty throughout his life. There were pictures of Uncle Marty with Karl and of course with me.

Uncle Marty loved me.

Mommy had pulled a muscle in her back and needed to sit down. T-Bone gave Leilani the task of making Mommy and me comfortable. She took her job seriously and put a pillow on a recliner for my mommy, got a soft bed for me, and even placed a bowl of water close by for me.

Then she made a drawing to show people that the chair was reserved for her grandma. I love Leilani!

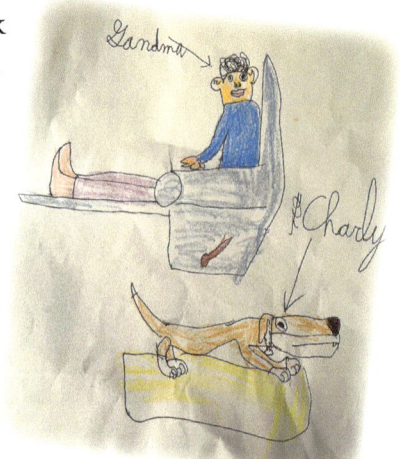

Leilani made a sign letting everyone know this special place was for me and Mommy.

Sign Language

May 17, 2023. Mommy has been teaching me a little sign language. Today she signed *Vest* and *Go for a ride*. The *Vest* sign means I'm going to work as Mommy's service-stability dog. Daddy usually puts my vest on, and I looked for him to come down the hallway; but then Mommy signed that she would get my vest. I always go wherever they go.

I love learning sign language.

Up!

May 23, 2023. I went to see my doctor to get my allergy shot, but first he wanted to see if I was my usual healthy self. Mommy told me to lie down as the doctor sat on the floor with me. He checked my teeth, ears, temperature, scar, and eyes, and then he began rubbing my head and pushing my hips, ribs, and chest. This went on for awhile like it was some ritual thing—until Daddy said, "Doctor, what are you doing?"

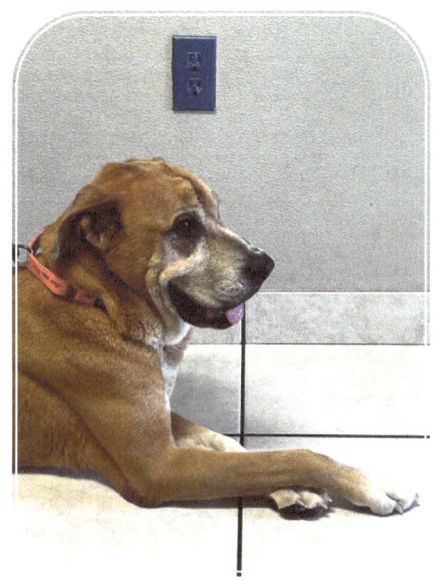

Waiting in Dr. Benish's office.

He said, "I'm trying to get Charley to stand up."

Mommy said, "That's easy. Charley, UP." Service dogs know lots of commands.

My doctor looked at Mommy and laughed as he said, "I could have told him that!"

Boots on the Ground

May 25, 2023. The pavement and sidewalks in Arizona can get so hot, they would burn my feet if I worked barefoot. While I was in training to be a service dog, Mommy ordered boots for me, and while they were on the way, she taught me to shake "hands." Every time I put my left paw up, she shook my paw and gave me a treat. She did this several times a day. Then she wanted my right paw. Okay. Either way, I got a treat. Then some red boots arrived, and Mommy said, "These are for you, Charley!"

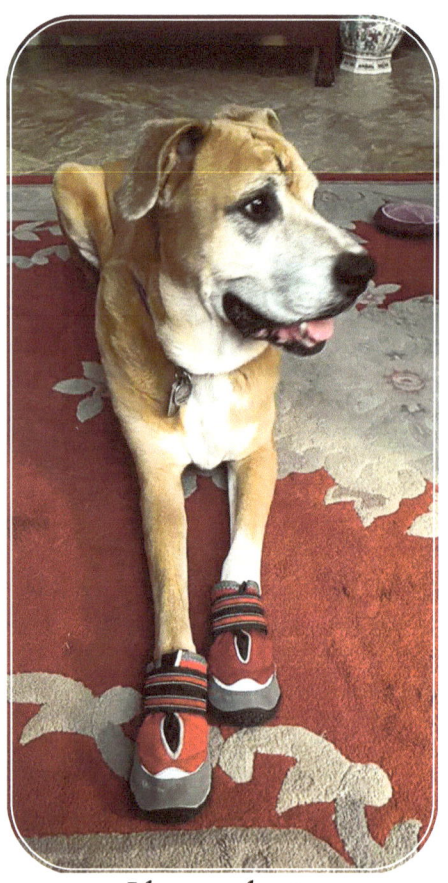

I love my boots.

We shook "hands," and I got a treat. Then she put the boot on my paw, and I got another treat. Then I walked around the TV room with the boot on my paw, and I kept getting treats. The next day she put on two boots. Same thing. I walked around in those two boots and got treats. The following day she put on four boots. I got a treat with each boot, and then I discovered they were kinda fun! They made a clopping sound when I walked. Daddy let me go outside with my boots on, and they gripped the grass and helped me to run faster!

Now that it's almost June and I have to help Mommy on the sidewalk, the cement is hot, and I must wear my boots. As Mommy puts each boot on before we go out, I get some beef jerky with each boot. When I see my boots, I sit and lift up each front paw to help her. I stand up when she puts my boots on my back feet. I love getting four treats.

Now that I'm a fully trained service dog, she puts my boots on and signs: *Get your vest on; we are going for a ride.* This means I get to go to work!

Perspective

May 27, 2023. I have always been a good boy. However, sometimes my mommy and daddy don't understand things from my perspective. So here's what really happened.

Daddy was getting ready to go to bed. He put his daytime clothes next to him on the bench in our bedroom and went to the big closet. That was my chance. When he turned his back, I took his T-shirt into the living room and laid down on it.

Daddy came back to the bench and said, "Sweetheart, where's my T-shirt?!" Mommy said she didn't know. Daddy came out to the living room and said, "Charley, why did you take my T-shirt?"

I rubbed my face on his leg to show him, "You smell so good, Daddy!"

A Visit to the Chiropractor

June 11, 2023. I went with Mommy and Daddy to the chiropractor's office today. Mommy has been teaching me sign language. When people see me they want to pet me, which isn't allowed, so Mommy tells them how to say "Hello" to me by putting two fingers to the corner of their eye, as they say, "Hello, Charley." When I see that sign, I look into their eyes with all the love I have in my heart. They always smile.

Today when I came into the doctors' office, the woman behind the desk came around to me and signed, "Hello." She was so happy when I looked into her eyes.

Then we went to another room and the doctor signed "Hello." She was also happy when I looked into her eyes.

People love it when I look into their eyes.

But then Mommy laid down on this table, and the doctor began pushing on her back. Sometimes Mommy said, "Ouch . . . Ouch . . . Ouch . . ." Well! I didn't like that, and I danced with my front paws and tried to go over to Mommy, but Daddy had a tight grip on my leash.

Then it was Daddy's turn. Good! As Daddy gave Mommy my leash, he said, "You will have to really hang onto him because he wanted to go over to you."

Mommy came back to the chair by me, and I was happy to have her back by my side. When Daddy was on the table, he was saying "Ouch," too. Well . . . he's on his own. I didn't pull on my leash at all because Mommy was with me, and all was right with the world.

Howling

August 19, 2023. Today we went out to lunch, and when we came out of the restaurant, a big firetruck was going past us. It was honking its horn, and it had a screaming siren! The sound stirred my doggy heart. I stopped walking, lifted my head, and let out a *howwwlll!* I heard the call of my ancient ancestors. Then another big firetruck sped by. I had to stop again and lift my nose to the sky and *howwwlll!* Of course, I was next to Mommy, and she was smiling at me. And then a third truck went by. It was even louder than the first two. I let out another *howwwlll!* Letting out that sound felt so good. When I looked at Mommy again, she was smiling as she touched my face and said, "Charley, the sound you made was beautiful."

Mirror, Mirror

August 23, 2023. Today Mommy took me with her into the restroom in the restaurant so she could wash her hands, and I saw a dog in the mirror by the sinks. I was so scared! Who was this dog with no smell staring right at me? That is not polite doggy behavior. I ducked down by the sink and looked up again . . . That dog was still there! I was so happy to leave the restroom. Mommy said that the dog was me! How was I supposed to know I was looking at myself? At least I didn't bark or growl. That would have been embarrassing! I think mirror training should be added to service dog training.

At Work?

*Mommy thinks this is funny.
I don't.*

November 30, 2023. I sure hope Mommy was joking when she created this picture of what I'm going to look like in my new work clothes. Some things just aren't funny.

*Please say you
were joking, Mommy.*

Prince

December 3, 2023. Mommy says I'm the prince of service dogs. It's not easy sleeping with a crown on my head, but whatever makes Mommy happy.

*Mommy calls me the
Prince of Service Dogs.*

A Challenge

January 14, 2024. The other day, Mommy, Daddy, and I went to a popular restaurant, and as usual I was wearing my vest with its bold words: SERVICE DOG. DO NOT PET. As we were leaving the restaurant, a mother and her mentally challenged son were waiting to enter. The boy was clearly terrified of me and started waving his hands and yelling, "No, no, no, no!" My mommy froze, and I stood quietly by her side.

There were a lot of people also coming into the restaurant at this time. Everyone around us froze, too. No one knew what to do. In order to leave the restaurant, we would have to walk by the mother and her son and all the people entering the restaurant. It was a busy time of day.

I looked up at the mother with soft and loving eyes. She reached down, and ignoring the words on my vest, rubbed my face with both of her hands and said, "See, he won't hurt you." Then Mommy walked me past the mother and her son, and I was careful not to look at the young man. I sensed he was still a little scared of how big I was. As we walked through the crowded entryway, everyone smiled at me. Sometimes exceptions have to be made to the no petting rule.

A Taxing Day

March 4, 2024. It was a busy day today. After breakfast we went to the tax office where Mommy and Daddy talked to this tax person, then lunch, and then physical therapy with Mommy.

So here's the thing. Mommy says that I walk like a rock star, and even though my vest says "Service Dog. Do Not Pet," everyone wants to pet me and, well, Mom lets them pet me. She knows how handsome and irresistible I am. I've gotten used to all of these kind and gentle people petting me and smiling at me. Now I have expectations.

For example, every time I go to physical therapy with Mommy, people say, "Hi, Charley!" Apparently, they don't know Mommy's name. Then people pet me. And I've come to expect this kind of treatment.

This is my side of the story. Today we all went to an office where Mommy and Daddy talked and talked and gave this nice woman a bunch of papers. Mommy usually puts my leash under her leg, which keeps me in my place. But today she forgot to secure my leash. The door was open in this small office, and I was getting no attention from the lady behind the desk.

While I was lying on the floor for what seemed like six hours, I felt the need for some attention. I saw the end of my leash on the floor, and I got up and slowly sauntered out the door and into the hallway. I saw an open door in the hallway that opened into a room with several nice ladies who noticed me. They smiled and started talking to me. One woman even got up from her desk and came over to me. But then Daddy caught up to me and took me back to that boring room before anyone could give me the attention and petting I deserved.

Some days, my work life isn't that interesting. Sigh . . . I had to wait until Mommy's physical therapy appointment to get my fill of attention.

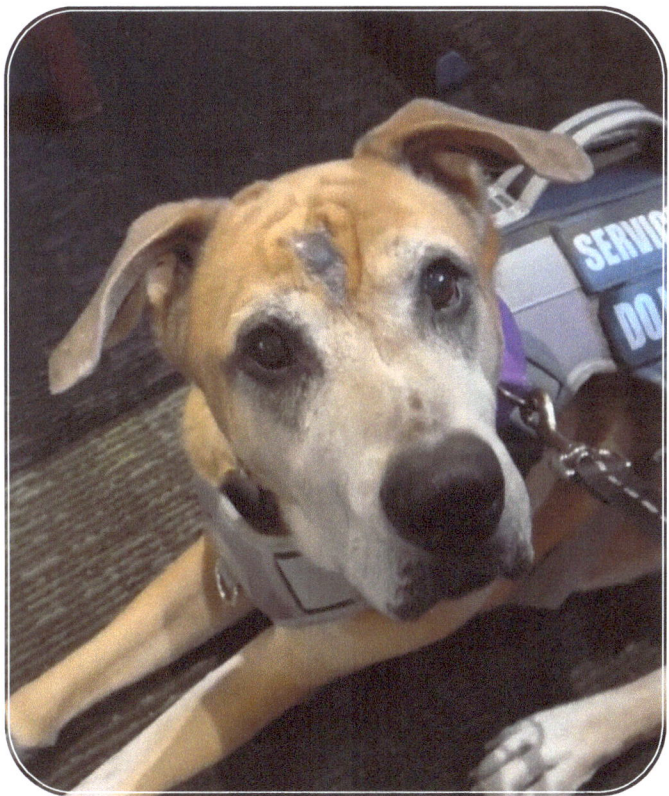

I have expectations.

Rock Star

March 17, 2024. As a service dog I wear a vest that says, "SERVICE DOG. DO NOT PET." However, since I'm a rock star, everyone wants to pet me. I love the attention.

So here's what happened. As Mommy and Daddy were eating breakfast at a restaurant, this kind lady kept staring at me. I looked back at her with my loving eyes. When we were leaving, she reached over and petted my face and ears as she said to my parents, "I can't read." That's just the way it is for rock stars!

Who can resist me?

A Visit to the Vet

May 24, 2024. I saw a nice doctor the other day. Of course, I had my service vest on, so my doctor knows I'm trained to be a good boy. My mommy told the doctor I had a little lumpy-bump on my foreleg and two on my back leg. I wasn't worried about it until my doctor left the room and came back with three big needles. Uh oh!

First, she told my mommy she was going to collect a few cells from the lumps to help her figure out what they were. Then she kneeled down next to me and petted me all over my face. She had kind and loving eyes. While I was thinking about her lovely eyes, she stuck a needle deep into my front leg—twice! I barely felt it, but I could feel her hair touching my ear, and that tickled.

Then she stuck the lumpy-bumps on my back leg. Mommy and Daddy were there watching, so I knew I was safe.

As the doctor got up off the floor, an assistant opened the door to our room and hesitated when she saw how big I was. I wagged my tail as the doctor said, "Don't worry about him. I had my head right by his mouth, and he didn't do anything."

Of course I didn't do anything. I'm a good boy.

A few days later my doctor removed the little lumpy-bumps, and while I was under anesthesia, her technician cleaned my teeth. I woke up with that cone on my head!

A week after having my lumpy-bumps removed, the doctor called Mommy and said all is well. An edge study showed healthy cells where the bumps were removed. I had sparkling white teeth, too!

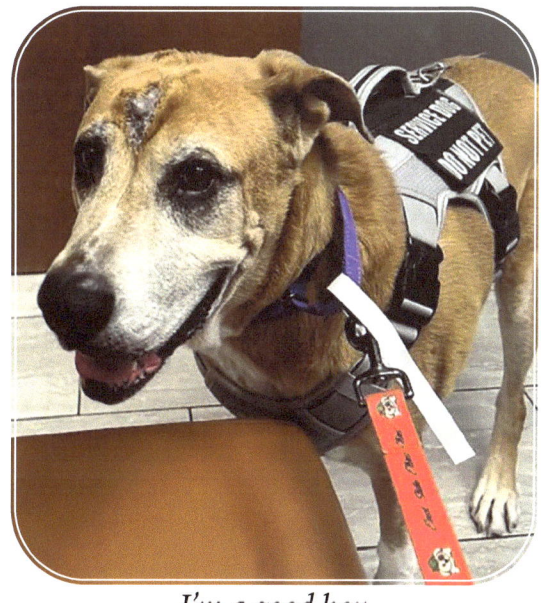

I'm a good boy.

A Working Dog

December 16, 2024. Mommy's hip was hurting so she had a doctor's appointment this morning. For a while we waited in a big room with lots of chairs. Daddy was there with us, too. Then some woman called Mommy's name, and Mommy and I left Daddy in the waiting room. He wasn't allowed to go with us.

I got extra practice today working with two of the many commands I know: *Turn right; Turn left.* Mommy used those two commands about six times. I felt like a rat in a maze!

Back when my trainer said I was ready to be certified as Mommy's service-stability dog, I thought my training was done. Nope! Since then, Mommy has taught me a lot more and reinforced all of the commands my trainer taught me.

Not to brag about what a good boy I am, but here are all the commands I know: *Sit, Up, Down, Come, Let's go, Wait, Stay, No, Yes, Back up, Go see, Where's Daddy, Tell Daddy you want dinner, Turn right, Turn left, Go straight, Shake* (paws), *Give me your paw* (so I can put your boots on), *Okay* (do what you want), *Get your vest on, Get in the car, Break* (training is done), *Look at me* (pay attention), *Go potty,* and *Go to your place.*

I know some hand signs, too: *Yes, No, Up, Down, Look at me, Good boy, Come, Go to place, Sit, Paw, Stay, Wait,* and *Get your vest on; we are going for a ride.* My favorite hand sign is: *Do you want some whipped cream?*

Mommy and Daddy only know one command from me. When I put my nose in their hand it means I want something. Then they have to guess what it is. It could be that I want dinner or a doggy cookie, or to go outside. It could also mean I want to go to work, or it's time for everyone to go to bed.

On this day, Mommy and I waited in another room, and then we were called again. Mommy and I walked into a big room with lots of scary machines. Mommy said it was an x-ray room.

There were two women in the room, and one of them told Mommy to turn right while the other woman took my leash and led me behind a big wall. I started to softly cry because I couldn't see my mommy. The woman said, "Your Mommy is okay, Charley. You can just look around the corner and see your Mommy, but you can't go in."

I peeked around the corner of the big wall and saw my mommy. She was okay, and I stopped whimpering.

The other woman was moving big machines around Mommy, and Mommy wasn't crying or anything, so I began to relax. There were strange clicking sounds, and I wondered if the women were trying to train Mommy with these big clickers. The two women were talking about something, but I didn't hear the word "dinner" or any other of my favorite words, so I figured whatever they were talking about wasn't important.

Mommy saw me peeking around the corner of the wall and said, "Stay, Charley. Good boy." And soon Mommy walked over to me, and the two kind women said, "Goodbye, Charley. You are such a good boy."

Then I heard more "Turn right . . . Turn left," and we went to another room where Daddy was waiting. Mommy and Daddy talked to a doctor for a little while in that small room. He said Mommy didn't break any bones. The doctor was nice to me, too. And then we got to go home. It's all in a day's work!

Firemen to the Rescue

December 21, 2024. It's been quite an adventure today. It was in the middle of the night when I felt a little thirsty. As I was walking to the kitchen to get a drink of water, I moved the wrong way, and the pain was the worst pain ever! I yelled out so loud, Daddy woke up and came over to me where I had collapsed in the living room. Daddy said, "What happened, Charley?!"

My front legs were shaking, and I showed Daddy that I couldn't get up. Daddy woke up Mommy. She came over to me and said, "Charley, you need to go to the emergency room." Mommy and Daddy couldn't lift me into the car because I weigh eighty-five pounds.

Mommy called the fire department. A fireman answered right away, and he said he would be right over in his firetruck.

Daddy brought out a large soft blanket, folded it in half, and put it on the floor next to me. Mommy put my vest on, which has a handle. Daddy pulled up on the handle and pulled me over and onto the blanket. When I was on the blanket, Mommy told me I was such a good boy. As she was petting me, Daddy unlocked the front door and then parked our car in the driveway.

Only minutes later the firetruck arrived. Four strong men jumped out of the truck and walked quickly to the door and inside our house. The men came over to me, and just as they each held a corner of the blanket and lifted me up, I stood up. I was scared! One man said to my mommy, "Could you tell him to lie down?"

Mommy was in front of me and gave me the hand sign for *Down*. As soon as I saw her hand sign, I laid down. Then she gave me the hand sign for *Yes* and said, "Good boy, Charley." The firemen quickly walked to the car and gently laid me down in the back seat. Daddy drove me to the hospital along with my mommy.

The emergency room doctor told Mommy and Daddy she would call after I had x-rays, and she knew what was wrong with me.

After my x-ray, the doctor gave me an injection of methadone. Let me tell you . . . that is some powerful stuff! I was able to limp around after that.

A few hours later I was back home. I have tendinitis in my shoulder. The doctor told Mommy to put me on sick leave from work for awhile. Mommy said she didn't want to go anywhere without me, so she would just stay home with me.

I had my dinner tonight, some pain pills, and now we are all going to bed. All is right with the world. AND Mommy is sending a tin of cookies to everyone at the firehouse!

Bigger Bed, Please

February 3, 2025. I need a bigger bed. When we have our family meeting, I'll be mentioning this small bed.

This new bed is too small.

It Was a Dead Duck

April 2, 2025. T-Bone and Angie volunteer with an organization called Guide Dogs for the Blind. They help out when a puppy-in-training needs some training for a few days, and the regular trainer needs some time off. T-Bone and Angie were taking care of a young service dog and brought her over to my house! And without my permission, too.

So here's what happened. T-Bone brought a young guide dog over. Her name is Teal. (What was someone thinking? Naming a dog after a color?! I'm going to name her Purple, just because I can.) So, Purple brought her green duck with her to my house. Then she left her duck all alone while she went outside. As soon as I saw her lonely duck, I took it! Losers, weepers, and I'm gonna keep her! Or something like that.

This is my duck now!

The Nose Knows

May 1, 2025. Part of my job as my mommy's service dog is to make sure she is safe on sidewalks, parking lots, doorways—anyplace she wants to go. The way I check these places is with my nose. I also check people this way, too, to see if they are a good person. I take a little sniff in the air, and I just know.

Not to brag or anything, but I can sniff something that is a football field away. I can hear really well, too; like I can hear my mommy's heartbeat. I always know how she is feeling.

Anyway, today Daddy dropped us off in front of our favorite breakfast restaurant, and I had to help Mommy up a curb so we could get to the door of the restaurant. When Mommy said, "Okay," that meant I should get out of the car.

I jumped down and sniffed the asphalt in the parking lot. Everything was okay, and then I walked Mommy to the curb. Just then, two people walking down the sidewalk toward us—probably a husband and wife— stopped and waited as they watched me work. Maybe they knew that working dogs always have the right of way.

When Mommy and I got to the curb, I started smelling the curb. I always do this. Mommy saw the couple watching me. Because they were puzzled by my sniffing, Mommy said, "He's a retired bomb sniffing dog."

They laughed as the wife said, "Let us know if he finds a bomb!"

It's all in a day's work for me.

Magical Place

May 17, 2025. Mommy is supposed to start making lunch at 11:00, but she was doing other things today, so I followed her around the house and kept putting my nose in her hand. Finally! At 12:30 she went into the kitchen. That's my signal to go to my magical place. This is the place where I get pieces of London broil just by sitting there! It's just outside the kitchen. But, if I go one paw closer to the kitchen when Mommy is making lunch, I don't get squat!

My magical place just outside the kitchen.

Smookums

June 28, 2025. Lately I've had smookums in my eyes, and my doctor gave Mommy some antibiotic eye drops for me that help my eyes a lot.

When Mommy or Daddy see smookums in my eyes they'll say, "Come here, Charley. You've got smookums." They gently wipe my eyes and give me a piece of doggy beef jerky. So yummy. Sometimes they also put the drops in my eyes.

Leilani was over at my house and Leilani said, "Grandma, Charley has stuff in his eyes."

Grandma said, "Charley, come here. You've got smookums."

Mommy wiped my eyes and gave me a treat as Leilani watched. Then Leilani said, "Why does Charley have smookums?"

Just then Leilani's mother came into the room smiling and said, "Is Grandma teaching you bad words?"

Leilani wasn't sure but said, "Yes."

Leilani's mother said, "What word did she teach you?"

Leilani said, "Smookums."

Leilani's mother laughed and said, "You can say that word."

Every time I hear that word, I get some beef jerky. Where's my treat?!

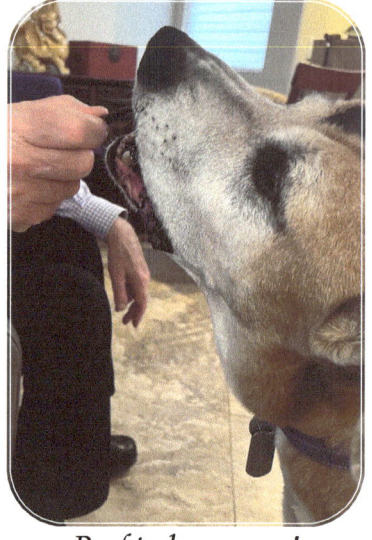

Beef jerky—yum!

A Little OCD With My TLC

July 7, 2025. I love arranging my toys in patterns—lines, diamonds, and squares—and it's even better if their shapes also match. In the TV room, I never bother to watch TV, but from my big raised bed I do like to keep an eye on my toys.

Mommy said I have a little OCD, and when I looked puzzled, she said it meant *obsessive compulsive disorder*. None of those words sounded familiar to me, but I think she means that I'm very good at paying attention to detail. That's what makes me such a great service dog.

In return, Mommy and Daddy give me TLC. I do know what those words mean: *tender loving care.*

Three of my favorite toys.

I don't like my toys to feel lonely.

Mommy says I just have OCD.

Language of Behavior

July 11, 2025. So here's the thing. Mommy and Daddy had baked salmon wrapped in bacon and asparagus with a little butter for lunch. AND there were leftovers! Mommy put the leftovers, with a piece of bacon only an inch long, in my bowl. The aroma was delectable!

"Mommy when am I going to get my snack of asparagus, bacon, and salmon?"

Holy moly! I've never tasted this smell. I heard doggy angels singing, "Charley, you will love this."

"Mommy, when can I have my snack?!"

Mommy told me to heel, and we went to the opposite side of the house, far away from my bowl—my delectable snack I have never had before! The doggy angels were getting annoying now with their singing, "Charley, you will love this," like mosquitoes buzzing in my ear.

After we got to the other side of the house, I walked on my own back to the kitchen but Mommy had put my bowl up so high, I could only smell how good it was going to be.

Mommy then did that whole routine again. And I went back into the kitchen to get my reward! Drat! The doggy angels were not only singing but inviting their other angel friends to watch. Sigh . . . When can I have my snack?!

Mommy took me to the other side of the house two more times! Each time I went back to the kitchen for my snack.

Then she said, "I give up." The smells of my snack taunted me. The doggy angels wouldn't stop their singing.

Then Mommy went to the big freezer in the back of the house. I went with her. "Mommy, how long do I have to wait for my snack?!"

Her answer? She took out an ice cream bar with chocolate all over it—which I know is not for me. I asked her again, "Mommy, when can I have my snack?!"

She said, "Charley, behavior is a language."

What does that mean?! Somebody help me!

Mommy sat in her chair and ate her ice cream bar right in front of me, so I drooled all over the legs of her pants. How do you like them apples, Mommy?! I think it took her an hour to eat that ice cream bar. Finally she said, "Charley, let's try again."

This time I stayed right by Mommy's side while we walked far, far away from my snack. Then I sat down. Then I stayed while Mommy walked away. Then I came to Mommy when she said, "Come." Then, when I was right in front of my bowl, she told me to "WAIT!" A guy can only take so much! There was an army of doggy angels now. They were all singing: "Good boy, Charley!" THEN Mommy said, "Go see!" That meant whatever was in my bowl I could have. Wowzah! That snack was the best.

Complete Circle

July 31, 2025. A long time ago, like in 2023, we all went to a Homeowner's Association Meeting at the library. Boring! Once Mommy and Daddy were seated, I stretched out by Mommy's feet. Because I'm so big, I was halfway in the aisle by the door when some women walked in and one of them said, "That's the dog!"

I looked at her, and it was Brittie! She was the kind woman who found me lost and wandering in a park. She took me to her home and then to a doctor who said I had no chip. I had no collar, either. She took me back to her home where she took a picture of me and put it on her refrigerator.

Brittie and her husband Jesse were sad for me because I was lost and scared. They did not know where my home was.

The next day, when the homeless shelters for dogs were open, Jesse took me to the Maricopa County Care and Control shelter for dogs. Lucky for me, I was adopted two months later.

At the meeting at the library, Brittie was so happy to see me. She explained to my Mommy and Daddy who she was. My mommy hugged her and thanked her for saving me from the streets. Brittie saw my service dog vest and could see I was healthy, happy, and living the good life.

Mommy was talking to Brittie on the phone today. She told her again how much she appreciated Brittie and her husband Jesse for saving me. Mommy said, "We couldn't love Charley more."

That's true, and I couldn't love Mommy and Daddy more.

The "Look"

August 10, 2025. This is the look I give Mommy when I want to play a game. One of my games is called "Go Find It!" Mommy hides treats around the house while Daddy makes me stay in another room. Then Mommy says, "Charley, go find it!"

Wowzah! That's when there is dust behind my paws, and my nose is to the ground like a road grader. When I find a treat and she says, "Go find it" again, that means there are more treats somewhere. When she says, "Break," that means I found them all. Game over . . . Sigh. I wait for a while, and then I give Mommy the look again, but the game is truly over. Mommy says I'm an eighty-five pound chow-hound. But Uncle Will approves.

Uncle Will was one of my trainers who taught me how to be a real service dog. He wrote a book about the power of doggy noses called *Sniff to Soothe*. That's how Mommy and I learned to play "Go Find It." This book will make life more fun for a whole world of lucky doggies. I love Uncle Will.

If I look at Mommy long enough,
she will play a game with me.

Note from Mommy: Look on Amazon.com for *Sniff to Soothe: Rewiring Neurobehavioral Patterns of Aggression, Anxiety, and Reactivity Through Structured Scent Work* by Will Bangura.

[Not] The End

August 31, 2025. Charley (still) here. As we close this chapter, my greatest wish is for every sentient being to receive as much love as their heart can hold, and to find happiness in each day. Thank you, Karl, for bringing me into this story and helping to heal Mommy's heart. In these simple moments—filled with treats, laughter, and gentle words—all is right with the world.

I'm always watching you, Mommy.

Bonus  Stories and Interviews

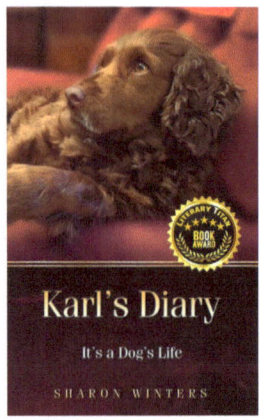

*hardcover, softcover,
eBook, audiobook*

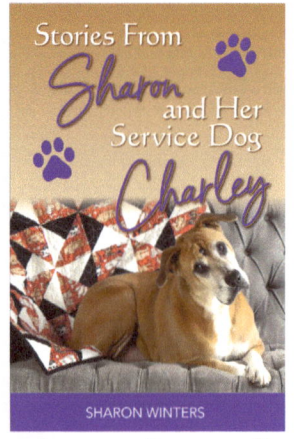

hardcover, softcover, eBook

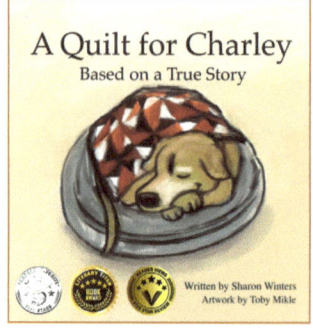

*hardcover, softcover,
eBook, audiobook*

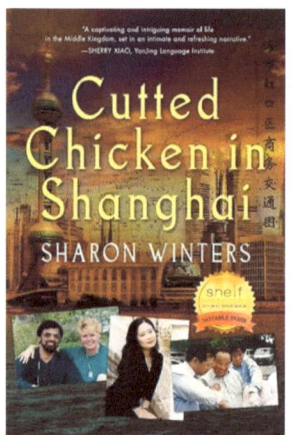

hardcover, softcover, eBook

hardcover, softcover, eBook

About Sharon Winters' Books

Before Charley, there was Karl . . . .

Karl's Diary: It's A Dog's Life

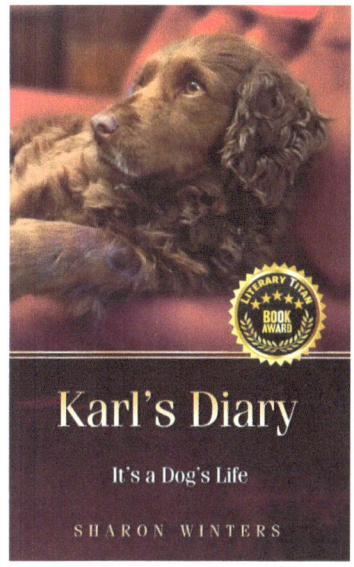

A kind-hearted man brought a lost dog to a rescue facility. Sadly, no one chose to adopt the stray, a handsome Boykin Spaniel whose desperate wish was for a family to love and cherish him. But when he moves to a second animal rescue, his picture is published in a local paper, and this leads to a life in a new home with Sharon Winters and her husband. Unconditional love, new doggy friends, and amazing meals are all part of Karl's wonderful new life.

Told from Karl's perspective, this book achieved Amazon #1 Bestseller status, and received the Literary Titan Gold Book Award granted to well-written books with great stories.

Not all of Karl's stories and pictures made it into *Karl's Diary*. This previously unpublished story on the next page, which was discovered in an old file, will delight readers who couldn't get enough of Karl, and win new hearts for those who want more.

Sharon Winters' books are available for sale on Amazon, Barnes & Noble, Apple iBooks, Kobo, Nook, Google Play, and other online bookstores. To connect with Sharon and learn more about her work:

https://SharonWinters.com
https://www.facebook.com/SharonWintersAuthor
https://www.instagram.com/sharon.winters.319

Bonus Story: Karl's Dinner

Karl here: One time on a visit to my doctor, he mentioned I could stand to lose a few pounds. I said the same thing to him, but he didn't hear me. Mommy told me to behave.

After that visit Mommy said she was going to feed me what she feeds Daddy. That night I had lettuce, organic beef *au jus*, and organic sweet potato. Mommy rubbed salt-free butter on the sweet potato skin and slow baked it. She drained off the butter before she put the sweet potato in my bowl, but she poured the beef juice over my lettuce.

When Daddy and Mommy took me back to the doctor for my annual visit, the doctor patted my neck and said, "Karl, you lost three pounds!"

I gave the doctor my sweetest look and said, "I'm sorry I can't say the same for you." The doctor didn't hear me. Mommy told me to behave.

The doctor asked my daddy about my diet, and after Daddy finished explaining, he added, "And I get Karl's leftovers."

Ha! What leftovers?!

Beef, lettuce, and sweet potato. Yum!

I love to watch from the kitchen entrance while Mommy fixes my dinner. Preparing my food looks very complicated.

A Quilt for Charley: Based on a True Story

The end of *Karl's Diary* is the beginning of Charley's story, another stray dog who found his forever home—and a job!—with Sharon Winters and her husband.

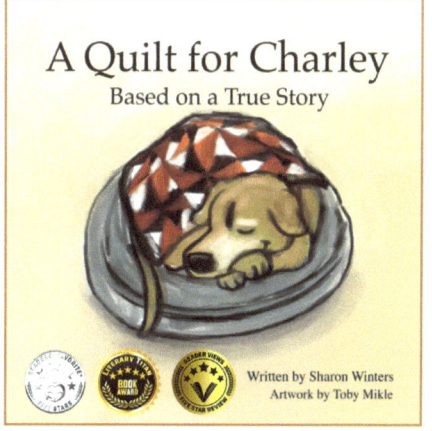

Sharon first wrote Charley's story as an illustrated children's book, *A Quilt for Charley: Based on a True Story*, about an older large dog that Sharon rescued from a local shelter to become her service animal. It is told from Charley's point of view. With a hugely satisfying ending, this book shows how a scared, lonely shelter dog adapts to his new life.

Winner of the Literary Titan Gold Book Award,
the Readers' Favorite Five Star Award, and
the Reader Views Silver Medal Reviewers Choice Award.

There is much more to Charley's life than could be shared in a children's picture book, which led Sharon to expand his story through a book written for adults: *Stories From Sharon and Her Service Dog Charley.*

Runtie the Desert Rat

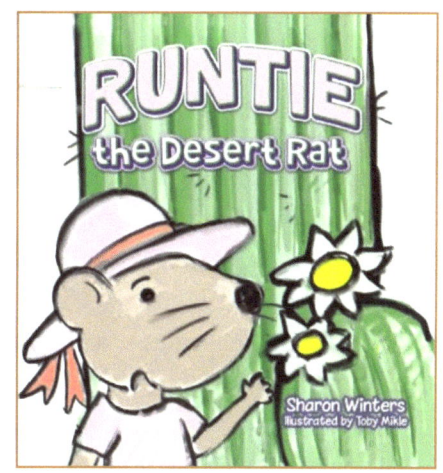

Sharon Winters wrote *Runtie the Desert Rat* for her young granddaughter. This children's picture book tells a touching story about a little animal with a big problem to solve.

Leilani is a desert rat who wonders if she'll ever grow as big as her older brothers and sisters. She wants to be able to run as fast as they do and find as many seeds as they can. But what can Leilani do to change her size? As she learns what it means to never give up, the lovable Leilani enchants and delights the hearts of all who encounter this brave desert creature.

With beautiful illustrations and whimsically wonderful characters, *Runtie the Desert Rat* brings the natural world to life as Leilani explores the vast landscape of the desert. Leilani's story examines what it's like to feel different, and helps readers both big and small to remember how truly magical the world of nature can be.

Cutted Chicken in Shanghai

When Sharon Winters and her husband moved to China for his job, she found humor and adventure, while her Shanghai driver, who didn't speak English, tried to keep her out of trouble. From supermarkets to restaurants, every aspect of her daily life offered a new lesson.

Part travelogue, part love letter, Sharon's memoir captures the humor, heart, and unforgettable adventures of living abroad, exploring culture, and finding friendship in a city that became her second home.

In *Cutted Chicken in Shanghai*, Sharon takes readers along on her daily adventures as she interacts with Chinese people and delights in both the similarities and differences she uncovers. As Sharon immerses herself in an unfamiliar culture, her quick wit, humor, and open heart endear her to those she meets, and her Chinese friends become as unforgettable to her as the China she comes to love. Interspersed with snapshots from her past, this book is an opening into the Middle Kingdom where there is something deeply familiar at its core.

Excerpt from an interview with Book Excellence
(www.bookexcellence.com)

Tell us about *Cutted Chicken in Shanghai*.

People often ask me, "What was it like to live in Shanghai?"

In *Cutted Chicken in Shanghai*, I invite you to step into my world as an American navigating life in one of the most fascinating cities on earth. Drawn from the journals I kept during my years abroad, this memoir is a candid, humorous, and heartfelt journey through culture shock, connection, and discovery.

From deciphering menus and braving chaotic supermarkets to relying on my driver (who didn't speak English) to keep me safe, every day brought new challenges and unexpected joy. But what I found most unforgettable were the friendships that blossomed along the way, reminding me that beneath cultural differences lies something universal: love, laughter, and belonging.

More than a memoir, *Cutted Chicken in Shanghai* is a love letter to the people who opened their hearts to me, and an invitation for you to find a piece of your own heart in a city that became a second home to me.

How did your background and experience influence your writing?

My fascination with other cultures has shaped both my life and my writing.

I hold a BA in psychology, sociology, and anthropology, and an MA in humanities: the study of culture itself. My professional experience spans teaching English 101 and special education, as well as working as an editor, all of which honed my ability to tell stories that connect with readers.

That lifelong curiosity, combined with my academic and professional background, informs the humor, heart, and insight woven into *Cutted Chicken in Shanghai*.

What is one message you would like readers to remember?

Living in Shanghai and being able to speak Mandarin transported me into a world where I had eleven million friends. One of my friends even gave me a Chinese name: Wen Li Xia, meaning *Warm Beautiful Sunrise*. Through the everyday adventures of shopping for art, pearls, and my husband's favorite cookies, I came to love not just the city, but its people and their rich, fascinating culture. I hope readers take away the joy of connection across cultures and the warmth that comes from embracing a world beyond their own.

Cutted Chicken in Shanghai has received positive reviews from well-known literary organizations, authors, and reviewers around the world. Book Excellence writes, "*With sharp wit and vivid storytelling,* Cutted Chicken in Shanghai *captures the humor, culture shock, and wonder of daily life in one of the world's most dynamic cities.*" In addition, Foreword Reviews writes, "*A delightful and . . . humorous marriage of memoir and travelogue.*"

First published in 2014, *Cutted Chicken in Shanghai* was republished in 2024 with a striking new cover and interior design.

Awarded 2014 Best Indie Book from Shelf Unbound

About Sharon Winters' Writing

Authority Magazine Interview with
Sharon Winters, November 2025

Authority Magazine (https://medium.com/authority-magazine) is an online magazine featuring in-depth interviews that draw out stories both empowering and actionable.

Can you tell us a bit about your 'backstory' and how you got started?

My youngest years were spent in Chicago, and during the day I was with caretakers who escaped from Poland after Hitler invaded. I was fascinated that they spoke English, Yiddish, Russian, and Polish. At the age of four my family moved to a German-Italian neighborhood. I was intrigued by people speaking languages I had to learn to understand.

Can you share the most interesting story that occurred to you in the course of your career?

When I was around eight years old, my father took me to a Chinese restaurant in Chicago where there were Chinese newspapers. My father handed me a newspaper, and as I looked at it, that driving curiosity came back to me, that curiosity to understand what people were saying. I asked my father to tell me what the newspaper said, and he didn't know. It was then that I said, "I want to learn Chinese and live in China," and he said, "Then you will." And I did live in China and learn Chinese. The newspaper was a spark that changed my life. I find people fascinating.

What was the biggest challenge you faced in your journey to becoming a writer? How did you overcome it? Can you share a story about that that other aspiring writers can learn from?

The biggest challenge for most writers is a blank piece of paper. When I lived in Shanghai I bought a journal and wrote something in it every day. Instead of staring at white paper, I brought up a picture in my mind and described it in writing. This journal became my first book: *Cutted Chicken in Shanghai*. Describing a picture becomes a story, and stories become a book.

It has been said that our mistakes can be our greatest teachers. Can you share a story about the funniest mistake you made when you were first starting? Can you tell us what lesson you learned from that?

I was working as an editor and creative art director for a publishing company in Dallas, Texas. Applying for a job with Intel Corporation, I wrote a cover letter and said I had experience as a "sopy" writer. Always proofread your writing—especially when you are a copywriter.

In your opinion, were you a "natural born writer" or did you develop that aptitude later on? Can you explain what you mean?

I discovered I could write when I was hired as a creative art director for a magazine publishing company, and one day I was suddenly an editor for three magazines. I had to write articles and stories, and I discovered that I could write. Because I found people fascinating, I asked interesting questions, which resulted in interesting stories and articles. Fascination is everywhere: the who, the what, the where, the how, the why. I've got to know. Curiosity is a demon chasing me!

What are some of the most interesting or exciting projects you are working on now?

I've just finished my fifth book: *Stories from Sharon and Her Service Dog Charley*. This book is a compilation of stories about interesting happenings with people, dogs, bees—things that happened to me and other curiosities. Not only am I curious about people, but animals, too, because they have a language of their own. I use my imagination to read their behavior and form pictures in my mind, which I translate into English. I used imagination to write three of my books. I see behavior from my dogs Karl or Charley, form a picture, and write about what I see in my mind. Sometimes I just see a picture, like when I wrote *Runtie the Desert Rat*. The question I was curious about was: How did a Desert Rat become a Kangaroo Rat? Using my imagination to write this children's book answered this question for me.

Here is the main question of our interview. Based on your experience, what are the "5 Things You Need To Be A Successful Author or Writer?" Please share a story or example for each.

1. CURIOSITY: Maybe I should say, be nosy. I was riding in a taxi, and the driver had an Arabic accent. Prayer beads in his taxi told me he was most likely a Muslim. I was nosy and said, "I heard Muslims don't like dogs."

He said, "Oh no, that's not true. Muhammad fell into a well, and when a dog heard him call for help, the dog found people to get Muhammad out of the well."

I have a "Two Foot Rule." If you are two feet away from me, I might talk to you. I want to know things. The world is a friendly place.

2. IMAGINATION: I wonder about something and then if there is no factual answer, I'm left to my imagination, and "I WONDER?!" I wondered if a Kangaroo Rat was first a Desert Rat.

A picture came to mind, and the pictures became the story: *Runtie the Desert Rat*. And I wondered what my dog Karl was thinking. I watched his behavior, looked into his eyes, and out of my imagination came: *Karl's Diary: It's a Dog's Life*.

3. HEAR PICTURES: As I go through my day, pictures are left in my mind. To my husband's dismay, I remember what words go with each picture. I can then describe these pictures, repeat all the words that go with them, and stories are born. *Cutted Chicken in Shanghai* consists of about 150 stories that originally started out as pictures I described in a journal. As a writer, I then described these pictures and repeated the words I heard so well that the reader can be transported to the places I have been and the people I have met—even when they are speaking another language.

4. FIND THE FUNNY: I have been told I have a wicked sense of humor. I have a "Rascal" that sits on my shoulder that no one can see, and he tells me what to say or do because, as my Rascal says, "Oh, that will be funny!" Sometimes the joke is on me, and those are the funniest happenings of all. Who doesn't like to laugh?

5. THE FIFTEEN MINUTE RULE: The best advice I ever got came from a counselor in high school. I told her I wanted to drop a class. She said, "Could you study for just fifteen minutes a day?" Of course I could do that, and that advice is what I apply to anything I want to put off: playing a difficult piece on the piano, a new quilt pattern I'm having a problem with, AND writing.

What is the one habit you believe contributed the most to you becoming a great writer? (i.e. perseverance, discipline, play, craft study). Can you share a story or example?

Writing is a process that has its own time. It teaches patience. It has a life of its own. The writing process I use is: 1. I have a topic I would like to write about. 2. I start with a picture in my mind—a scene I can see clearly. 3. I write about this picture. 4. I put the picture aside and read what I wrote. Does this writing describe what I hear and see? I reread it two or three times. 5. Sometimes I post this writing on my personal Facebook page. 6. I'm done writing for the day. 7. I keep writing these bits and pieces until there are no more pictures and there is a final scene.

Which literature do you draw inspiration from? Why?

My favorite writer is Pulitzer Prize-winner Russell Baker and his 1982 autobiography: *Growing Up*. Everyone's life has twists and turns. The life we planned is seldom the life we are living. Russell Baker's writing is personal and direct. His life had a theme: Make something of yourself. And he did. I wrote a letter to him telling him how much I enjoyed reading his book. He wrote back to me and mentioned how happy his mother was that he made something of his life. If I had to say what the theme of my life is, the theme would be: What were you thinking?!

If you could start a movement that would bring the most amount of good to the most amount of people, what would that be?

Get your teacher's license and teach in special education.

Sharon Winters' books are available for sale on Amazon, Barnes & Noble, Apple iBooks, Kobo, Nook, Google Play, and other online bookstores. To connect with Sharon and learn more about her work:

https://SharonWinters.com
https://www.facebook.com/SharonWintersAuthor
https://www.instagram.com/sharon.winters.319

Thank You for Reading
Stories From Sharon and Her Service Dog Charley

If you enjoyed *Stories From Sharon and Her Service Dog Charley*, I would be deeply grateful if you took a moment to share your thoughts in an Amazon review by scanning this QR code or going to this link: https://www.amazon.com/review/create-review?&asin=B0FYK7YPCV

Please leave a review for *Stories From Sharon and Her Service Dog Charley*. Your review makes a meaningful difference. Reviews not only help other readers find books they will enjoy reading and gifting to others, they also promote the love to be shared in adopting and training a shelter dog.

It doesn't have to be long or formal. Just a few sentences about what you enjoyed will help others decide if this book is right for them.

With gratitude,

Sharon Winters and Charley

www.ingramcontent.com/pod-product-compliance
Lightning Source LLC
Chambersburg PA
CBHW040855120626
46551CB00001B/31